Knowing God the Right Way
Reverend Robert Scales, III

Copyright © 2006 by Jesus is the Answer Ministries, Inc.
Revised 2009 – All Scripture Passages are King James Version unless otherwise noted.

ISBN-13: 978-0-9793939-0-7
ISBN-10: 0-9793939-0-6

Printed in the United States of America

Permission to reproduce or transmit in any form or by any means, electronic or mechanical, including photocopying and recording, or by any information retrieval system, must be obtained in writing from the author.

Call or write to:
Jesus is the Answer Ministries Inc.
P.O. Box 292112
Nashville, TN 37229
www.robertscalesministries.org
615-641-3505

TABLE OF CONTENTS

Introduction 1

Chapter 1 – Jesus Revealed in Us 3

Chapter 2 – Followers of Jesus 29

Chapter 3 – You Must Decide 67

Chapter 4 – The Love of God 93

Chapter 5 – Jesus - The Picture of God 115

Prayer 137

INTRODUCTION

Jesus is right and everybody else is wrong!

In 1998 the Lord Jesus appeared to me in a vision and taught me this message. I've been teaching it for eleven years now and I've never seen anything change people's lives as much as this message does. If you will meditate and apply these truths, you will be transformed into the image of Christ — you will walk like Him, talk like Him, think like Him, have power like Him, love like Him and forgive like Him. You will be all that Jesus wants you to be.

Many Christians do not believe that it is possible to be like Jesus, but we can because He commanded us to. Open your heart, be receptive, have your mind alert and when you finish this book you will not recognize yourself!

Unless you make the decision that the Word of God is always right and let it correct you, you will never grow in the Lord. You will always be just a learner. When you let the Word correct, instruct, reprove and rebuke you, God will teach you how to walk in His righteousness. When His Word rules your heart, He will turn you into the kind of man or woman of God that He has purposed you to be.

If you are not open and hungry for the truth, these will just be words; but if you will open your heart, be willing to learn, grow and be corrected, you will never be the same after reading this book. God will bring revelation and light to you. You will be able to take this truth and apply it to your life, and you will look more like Jesus than ever before.

Chapter 1

JESUS REVEALED IN US

But when it pleased God, who separated me from my mother's womb, and called me by his grace, to reveal his Son in me, that I might preach him among the heathen; immediately I conferred not with flesh and blood:
— *Galatians 1:15-16*

Paul was called of God by His grace. God didn't just call Paul; He called Him by His grace. Did you know that God has called *you* by His grace also? Just like Paul had this revelation, you too must know this. Why have we been called by His grace? The answer is found in verse 16. We have been called by His grace so that God's Son (Jesus) can be revealed in us. God wants to reveal Jesus in us.

Why do we need Jesus revealed in us? So we can preach Him among the unbelievers. The earth is dark and the only light available is the light of Jesus. The more Christ is revealed in us, the more we can shine in this world and bring unbelievers to the knowledge of Jesus Christ as their Savior. The less we know about Jesus, the less we will be able to. The more God can reveal Christ in us and how He loved us; the more we begin to act like Jesus becoming a light in this dark world. Unbelievers will see something different in us that they don't see in anyone else they know. Jesus stands out among everybody in the world.

Most Christians cannot win people to the Lord. They don't know how to witness. They don't know how to get people born again. They don't know how to love with the compassion of Jesus. But you can. If you grab hold of this message, it will change your life. When you walk in love, you will get so free you won't care what people think. You won't care what your family or anybody else thinks. Some people are afraid to witness; this is fear. They are afraid they will offend people. Jesus offended so many folks they wanted to kill Him. The love of God doesn't care what people think. If it did, Jesus wouldn't have offended so many people, but He did and never walked outside of love. Everything Jesus did was the love of God. Everything! Jesus did make the Jews mad. There will be times you have to tell people what God says and they aren't going to like it.

Jesus is to be revealed in us and to us. We cannot figure it out in our heads — our brains cannot dictate our walk with Christ. He wants us to walk in what He has revealed to us by the Holy Spirit. He never wants your brain, your feelings, or your intellect to have anything to do with your walk with Him. Less of you means more of Him. You can't confer with man to have Christ revealed in you. Now, a man can reveal Christ to you if the Holy Spirit has revealed Christ to him; but if he's not giving you what the Holy Spirit has revealed to him, then all you have is some intellect; flesh and blood.

What did Jesus ask His disciples in Matthew 16 when they were going to Philippi and Caesarea?

...Whom do men say that I the Son of man am?
— Matthew 16:13

What were their answers?

And they said, Some say that thou art John the Baptist: some, Elias; and others, Jeremias, or one of the prophets.
— Matthew 16:14

Jesus was really not interested in who the world thought He was. He was interested in who the people around Him thought He was.

He saith unto them, But whom say ye that I am?
-— Matthew 16:15

Look what Peter said in Verse 16.

And Simon Peter answered and said, Thou art the Christ, the Son of the living God.
— Matthew 16:16

That's knowledge. Let me break that down: You are the one that was sent from God. You are the one that was sent from Love. You are the one that came from heaven.

And Jesus answered in Verse 17,

...Blessed art thou, Simon Barjona: for flesh and blood hath not revealed it unto thee, but my Father which is in heaven.
— Matthew 16:17

Flesh and blood did not reveal it to Peter. We cannot receive the things of God unless they are revealed to us. We are not to use our brains to try to understand; we are to open our hearts and let the revelation come to us until we can say, "Oh, I see that now!" That's revelation knowledge.

Most Christians live in their brains. They use their intellect to try to know God with their physical senses and human thinking, and this is wrong. They don't really know God — they have experienced God, but they don't really know Him. The only thing you will ever get from God from your head is looking at the earth and knowing that God created it. That's the only thing you can get from your natural abilities — looking at His creation and knowing there is a God. Other than that, you can't know anything about God with your intellect. You don't really know God if you are using your intellect to try to know Him. If you are not interested in knowing God, there is something wrong. You have a problem when you do not want to know God. You should have a hunger and thirst to know Him because Jesus said in Matthew 5:6,

Blessed are they which do hunger and thirst after righteousness: for they shall be filled.
— Matthew 5:6

The rest of the people will sit in church and be learners. God will not reveal truth to them because He only reveals truth to those who hunger and thirst. He doesn't reveal it to anyone else. Just because you are in church learning, being nice, ushering, or doing some other work does not mean God is revealing anything to you. You can sit in church, be nice and do good works and still not know God; not know how to act like Him.

Now, how do you get Christ revealed in you? Here is what you must do first. This must become the most important area of your Christian walk, the most important thing in your life as a Christian. Look at Matthew 7:24.

Therefore whosoever heareth these sayings of mine, and doeth them, I will liken him unto a wise man, which built his house upon a rock:
— Matthew 7:24

In Luke 6, Jesus told the same story:

Whosoever cometh to me, and heareth my sayings, and doeth them, I will shew you to whom he is like: He is like a man which built an house, and digged deep, and laid the foundation on a rock: and when the flood arose, the stream beat vehemently upon that house, and could not shake it: for it was founded upon a rock.
— Luke 6:47-48

What is the rock? I can read this all day long, but if I don't know what the rock is, it means nothing. Most people say Jesus Christ is the rock. Some people say the Word of God is the rock, but both are wrong! Let me break it down. If the rock is Jesus Christ, you really can't take me somewhere with that. Where would you go with that? What does that mean? You can't go anywhere with that — it's not revelation. If the rock is the Word of God — I ask what Word? Take me somewhere with that! You don't go anywhere. What? Is the entire Bible the rock? No! That's not revelation.

Now, let's just go back and listen to Jesus, He tells us what the rock is. Isn't it better when Jesus tells us and we don't have to figure it out? We don't get to have any say in the matter. Jesus is always right. Matthew 7:24 says, "Therefore whosoever heareth these sayings of mine, and doeth them" — that's the rock. When you hear what Jesus Christ taught, said and did and do those things, you are built on the rock. You are not built on the rock when you simply hear Him. You are only on the rock when you hear Him and then do what He says to do.

Jesus never told us to follow the Bible. He told us to follow Him. He told us to keep His sayings and teachings. He didn't tell me I couldn't learn from the entire Bible, because the entire Bible from Genesis to Revelation is the counsel of God. It's the Word of God, but He didn't teach me to follow it. I don't follow Job. I don't follow David. I don't follow Moses. I don't follow Jeremiah. I don't follow Isaiah. I don't follow Joshua. I don't follow any of them. Now, I might learn something from all of them to help me follow Jesus, but if something in the Bible doesn't help me follow Jesus, I don't want it. I don't want Leviticus because I couldn't eat any shrimp, lobster or fried oysters! I couldn't have any bacon! I like fried, crisp bacon with eggs, biscuits and gravy! I like a little sausage and a little pork chops now and then! What about ribs? I like ribs on the grill! If you follow the Bible, you can't eat those things. So, I don't follow the Bible, I follow Jesus, because in Him I can eat all of this in moderation.

Most Christians have tried to follow the Bible instead of learning from it and following Jesus with their whole life. That's why there is so much junk in their lives. The only way to get rid of all that junk is to make Jesus right! My whole life is what Jesus said, what Jesus taught and what Jesus did.

Most Christians don't truly believe Jesus is right. Jesus taught in John 15:7.

If ye abide in me, and my words abide in you, ye shall ask what ye will, and it shall be done unto you.
— John 15:7

Jesus did not say anything here about the whole Bible. The letters of the New Testament had not yet been written, so He couldn't have been talking about reading Paul's writings. At one point, Peter and the other disciples were arguing about who was the greatest, so you know He sure wasn't talking about them! At that time, they had the Old

Testament and the books of the law — the books of Moses, but Jesus never pointed anyone to Moses. He said,

A new commandment I give unto you, That ye love one another; as I have loved you, that ye also love one another.
— John 13:34

Jesus did not tell us to keep the Ten Commandments. He told the Jews to do that. Sometimes Jesus wasn't even talking to us in the four Gospels. Sometimes He was talking to the Jews, the Pharisees and the Sadducees who were tempting Him and asking Him questions about the Law of Moses. These passages don't have anything to do with you and me. Remember, Jesus said in Matthew 7:24 that if you come to Him, hear His sayings/teachings, and do them, He will show you what kind of person you are going to be. You will come to the place where you will never be offended. I haven't been offended in over 12 years by anything or anybody. I never worry. I'm never depressed. Now, depression tries to come sometimes; thoughts will tell me I'm not going to make it, but I don't accept those thoughts because Jesus didn't teach me to be depressed. It's hard to be depressed when you are following Him. You just can't be depressed and stressed out when you follow Jesus because He never taught you to be like that. When you make Jesus your life, if He didn't teach it, say it, or do it on the cross for me — then I don't want it!

Look at Matthew 7:24 again. This revelation will last for eternity and change your life forever. Jesus said,

Therefore whosoever heareth these sayings of mine, and doeth them, I will liken him unto a wise man, which built his house upon a rock:
— Matthew 7:24

Now, why is this verse true? Because Jesus said it!

Now, look what Jesus said in John 14:6,

...I am the way, the truth, and the life: no man cometh unto the Father, but by me.
— *John 14:6*

Why is this true? Why is Jesus the way, the truth, and the life? Because Jesus said it! When you make this the truth — what He said — you can't accept anything else. Did you know that most Christians have never done this? They have never made Jesus right!

If we are following Him, why aren't we constantly saying, "Jesus said." "Jesus taught." "Jesus did." How can you follow someone and not imitate them? You have to talk about what they talk about all the time. You have to act how they act all the time. If you are really going to follow someone, you are supposed to be looking just like them, talking just like them, and walking just like them. Whatever Jesus had, we ought to have. If Jesus looked up, we ought to look up. If Jesus raised the dead, we ought to raise the dead. If Jesus healed the sick, we ought to heal the sick. If Jesus opened blind eyes, we ought to open blind eyes. Whatever the Master did, if I am following Him, I have the same power in me that He had to do the same works that He did so that I can look just like Him. I can love just like Him. I can forgive just like Him. I can forget how people have mistreated me and never hold it against them because Jesus told me I can.

Doubt will tell you that some folks are hard to love, but Jesus didn't tell you that! This kind of thinking will hinder you from walking with Jesus, but that's the way a lot of people think. You have your own ways about what you think and it has robbed you from your growth in Christ Jesus. You have to get rid of your ways and make Jesus right. You have to get His words abiding in you. Remember in John 15:7 Jesus said, "If you abide in me..." He never said, "If you abide in the Bible."

Jesus also made the following statements:

...I am the light of the world: he that followeth me shall not walk in darkness, but shall have the light of life.
— *John 8:12*

...If ye continue in my word, then are ye my disciples indeed; And ye shall know the truth, and the truth shall make you free.
— John 8:31-32

He goes on to say in Verse 36,

If the Son therefore shall make you free, ye shall be free indeed.
— John 8:36

Why is this true? Because, Jesus said it. It's not true for any other reason. You can't go back and check Jesus out. You can go back and check Moses and others out, but you can't go back and check Jesus out because He came from above. You have to believe that He came from God. Why? Because He said He came from God! That's the only way I know He came from God, because He said He came from God. How can you know He is the way, the truth and the life? You can't go anywhere to check that out — you have to believe that He was. You can't go back and question Jesus — you have to believe He was right and that every word He spoke was from God.

Let's continue in Matthew 7.

And the rain descended, and the floods came, and the winds blew, and beat upon that house; and it fell not: for it was founded upon a rock.
— Matthew 7:25

What's the rock? Hearing Jesus' words and doing them. That's the rock. When you act just like Jesus and obey His words, you don't fail. If you say the rock is the Word, where would you go with that? But, if you point me to what Jesus said, I know exactly where to look — Jesus' words — they are called The Red Words!

That's the rock. You don't see how you are, you see who He is. What He had you can walk in and stop walking in you. Aren't you tired of you? Your spouse might be saying, "I am! I'm tired of them acting ugly every week!"

And every one that heareth these sayings of mine, and doeth them not, shall be likened unto a foolish man, which built his house upon the sand: And the rain descended, and the floods came, and the winds blew, and beat upon that house; and it fell: and great was the fall of it.
— *Matthew 7:26-27*

Do you know what this means? You got mad because you didn't like what somebody did; you weren't keeping Jesus' commandment of loving the way He loved you! If you love the way He loved you, you forgive people when they are guilty, because when you were guilty Jesus died and forgave you.

But God commendeth his love toward us, in that, while we were yet sinners, Christ died for us.
— *Romans 5:8*

Jesus didn't die for you when you were right. He died and forgave you with His blood when you were wrong. He told you to go and love everybody else the same way. *You* can't live anymore and live this; you have to die! Most Christians haven't been willing to do this yet; really lay their lives down and follow Jesus with all their heart. They have done it in some areas, but in other areas they haven't.

Look at Matthew 7:24-26 in The New Living Translation.

Anyone who listens to my teaching and obeys me is wise, like a person who builds a house on solid rock. Though the rain comes in torrents and the floodwaters rise and the winds beat against that house, it won't collapse because it is built on rock. But anyone who hears my teaching and ignores it is foolish, like a person who builds a house on sand.
— *Matthew 7:24-26 (NLT)*

Now, here is the way — the only way — that you will get Christ revealed in you.

For I determined not to know any thing among you, save Jesus Christ, and him crucified.

— *I Corinthians 2:2*

Paul determined not to know anything except Jesus Christ and Him crucified. You have to make this same decision. You have to make a decision that you want to know Jesus Christ, and Him crucified more than anything else on this earth. Most Christians really have a sincere heart and a genuine love for Jesus; the best they know how, but most of the love they have for Him is feelings, not obedience to His commandments and teachings. It's their feelings, and it runs out when somebody does them wrong. They struggle, and I don't. How many people do you know that want to know the cross every day? Every day? Do you know anyone that wants to know Jesus and the cross every day? We've missed this. We haven't seen the revelation that Paul had about Jesus' teachings. Most people only choose to know Jesus Christ and they leave the cross out. Jesus doesn't want you to leave the cross out. Look at John 13:34 again.

A new commandment I give unto you, That ye love one another; as I have loved you, that ye also love one another.

— *John 13:34*

You can't obey this verse when you read it! Do you know why? Because this verse doesn't tell you *how* to do it, it only tells you *what* to do. It tells you to love the way Jesus loved you but how He loved you is not in the verse. There is no picture. The picture is on the cross. The "how to do it" is shown to us on the cross. If you try to live this verse without the cross, you are in your own flesh and thinking. He hasn't even shown you how He loved you until you look at the cross. Without the cross, people think that they *have* to love and forgive. No! People who think like that do not have the revelation — they are walking in their flesh and don't realize it. I don't *have* to love you. I don't *have* to forgive you. They don't realize that they have become a new creature — a love species — created in the same image as who was in Jesus. This is who you are today. All Jesus is telling you to do is to act like who He made you inside. It's not you having to do it. This is who you are. You are not your body anymore! You are not your thinking anymore! You are a new species that has never been on this earth before. You have a re-created spirit now that has the life and nature of God Almighty in it and He's not asking you to try to do this! He's telling you to live who you are now in Christ Jesus. God didn't love me in the Old Testament! I didn't have a covenant with God — He didn't do anything for me back then. I was in this world without God, with no hope, and without love. I had no forgiveness, I had no Redeemer, and I had no Deliverer. Israel had one, but nobody else on the earth did. I'm looking for the God that is in Jesus. I'm not trying to find Abraham's God. I want to learn the promises that God gave Abraham, but I'm after the God that was in Christ Jesus — that's the God that showed me love on the cross when I was dead wrong and guilty. I'm after Him.

I want to know Jesus because He's the one that loved me. When Jesus healed the woman with the issue of blood, He wasn't loving me. I might learn some principles from that, I can learn faith and get inspired by what she did that obtained her healing by her faith, but that's not Him loving me there. He was loving her. On the cross is where I see how He loved me. On the cross is where He healed me. On the cross is where He delivered me. On the cross is where He set me free. That's where I get my peace and joy. It's all about what Jesus did for me on the cross. I can learn from the entire Bible, but I've got to see the cross to see how He loved me.

Most Christians have never developed looking at the cross every day in every situation, seeing how they were loved so they will know exactly how Jesus wants them to act. This sets you free from ever being mad at people. You will quit being upset at things. I hardly ever get upset. I go ten months a year, never get mad at anybody, never get offended and people do me wrong. I never get offended — I just kill that mess. This is a decision people have to make.

Whenever you are mistreated, look at how Jesus treated you! Look at how you were guilty and see how He forgave you! He didn't say, "Well, I don't know about this one. You've been real ugly and acted real mean. You don't deserve this because you kept doing wrong a bunch of times." No! He went to the cross while we were messed up and we didn't even want to repent. We didn't even want to tell God we were sorry. Nobody repented. Nobody told God they were sorry. God's love doesn't wait until you say you are sorry. God's love loves you in order to give you a way to say you're sorry. God doesn't wait for someone to repent. God loved the whole world when nobody was sorry so that the world could repent and come to God through Jesus Christ. So when you love like Jesus, you don't wait on people to make it right. When you wait on people to say they're sorry, you're not loving like He loved you. He didn't wait on you.

You see how our thinking has gotten us all messed up? When we don't love like Jesus loved on the cross, we don't feel good about people anymore. Your wife might say, "Lord, why did you give me this man?" Sometimes she might look at you and say, "Dear God, what in the world did I get myself into?" But God has the answer. It's how He loved you in Jesus on the cross. God knows how to help you. How Jesus loved you on the cross is your answer.

When Paul said in I Corinthians 2:2, "For I determined not to know anything among you, save Jesus Christ, and him crucified," he knew this was the most important thing a Christian would ever walk in — We must know Jesus Christ first of all. The word "Christ" means "the Anointed One and His anointing." That's just knowledge, that's not revelation; because that comes from the Greek Concordance. So what would be revelation of the Anointed One and His anointing? It is who God is and what God did in Jesus. Your name is not who you are. Your name is what we use to identify you by. Who you really are is what you say and what you do. People have tried to make Jesus Christ be His title and not what He taught, said and did on the cross.

You can't determine not to know anything among you save Jesus Christ unless He said something. People are trying to know Jesus and don't even know what He said. It's crazy! They don't even know how He said to love — they just know His title. They say, "Oh, I know Jesus Christ," but they don't even know what He said. The Buddhists know what Buddha said. The Muslims know what Mohammed said. Christians ought to know what Jesus said!

So, when Paul said he was determined not to know anything among them except Jesus Christ — the One sent from God — how could he know the one sent from God? He would have to know what Jesus said and what Jesus taught. Let's break that down and look again at what Jesus said in John 13:34,

A new commandment I give unto you, That ye love one another; as I have loved you...
— John 13:34

That's Jesus Christ. That verse is Jesus Christ. That verse is not what we think about Jesus Christ, that verse *is* Jesus Christ. Him crucified is how to love like Him. This is how to obey that verse. That's why Paul said he had to know both — Jesus Christ *and* Him crucified. If I just know Jesus Christ and don't see Him crucified, I can't know how to obey what Jesus said. I've got to know both of them.

The New Living Translation says,

For I decided to concentrate only on Jesus Christ and his death on the cross.
— I Corinthians 2:2 (NLT)

The Lord is not going to decide that for you. You have to decide it. You have to decide to concentrate only on Jesus Christ and His death on the cross. That doesn't mean you don't have other things to concentrate on, but Paul was teaching that this has to be first in your life every day if you are going to walk in this truth. You must concentrate on this truth when you first wake up in the morning and it has to go on during the day and into the evening. It's got to continue when you get frustrated and when things go wrong. These scriptures are supposed to be popping up out of our spirits because we have Jesus' words living in us and we are following Jesus — we know what Jesus taught, said, and did, and we are determined not to know anything except Jesus Christ and Him crucified. Therefore, when someone makes you mad or mistreats you, Jesus' teachings rise up and say, "Remember how I did you? Remember when you were wrong and I forgave you?" And when those words come up on the inside of you, they will shut you up!

You have to give what was freely given to you *if* you have that picture to look at every day. Some people are in fellowship with God and they follow the inward witness, when He lets them know that something isn't right, but they still don't have the picture — they just get over things. You don't really get free and you don't grow if you aren't freely giving to others what Jesus gave to you. If you had that picture, you would immediately get over anything and at the snap of a finger it would be gone. You may grow and mature in some areas but if you don't mature in love you can't really mature as a Christian because the only thing that will make you spiritual is love. The gifts of the Spirit won't even make you spiritual! Thank God for the spiritual gifts — I believe in them — but they are not going to make you spiritual. They are not going to make you act like the cross.

When you act like the cross, you are spiritual. That's how you become spiritual. When you don't do anything wrong and others accuse you and persecute you and treat you like you did something wrong, and you don't open your mouth except to pray, "Father, forgive them for they know not what they do," then you are a spiritual person! Some Christians can't even handle someone pulling out in front of them — Honk! Honk! — and they shout, "Hey, where did you get your license?" I did that the first two or three years I was saved because I was a baby Christian, but I haven't done it since. After that, when someone pulled out in front of me and drove real crazy and feelings rose up, Jesus' teachings rose up within me saying, "Love like I loved you," and those feelings melted and I ended up growing and maturing through my obedience to Jesus' teachings.

Everyone will get opportunities to grow in love like this. You can go onto an island by yourself and a monkey will make you have to walk in love! You will have to walk in love no matter where you go. You can go swimming and you might have to forgive a shark for wanting to come over and bite you. You just can't get away from walking in love. Something will come against your love walk every day unless you hide somewhere by yourself! But even then, you will have to love you! Don't leave you out. You may start feeling bad about yourself, but you have to love no matter what. If you start thinking ugly about yourself and remembering things you used to do, that's not the cross. That's not how Jesus loved you.

Many Christians come up in the prayer line to get healed, and there is an anointing for that, but the main way to get healed is to love like Jesus loved you. That will heal you of anything. You can't have any yesterday if you love like Jesus. You can't even have a past if you love the way He loved you because when He loved you He knocked your past out. So if you can't remember how you've been mistreated, you can't be hurt. Hurt people remember how they have been treated — that's why they hurt. When you walk in love, you're not hurt, because you won't have any remembrance of what anyone did to you. You will not be afraid to give love because you are not looking to see if people are going to do right. God wasn't looking at who was going to do right down here — Love came and loved whether you were doing right or not. Love doesn't wait until people get right. Love comes and shows you the way that is right so you can follow it and you can be right.

When you are in fear, you are suspicious. You think, "I wonder if they are going to hurt me. If I show them love, I wonder if they will reject me. I wonder if they will be mean to me. I wonder if they will take advantage of me." The Lord doesn't think like that. Love doesn't think — it just acts like Jesus on the cross. Love doesn't have a brain. It passes your knowledge. When you know the love of Christ, it passes your brain, your intellect. If you go upstairs in your head, you will not love like Jesus.

Look at I Corinthians 2:2 in the New Living Translation again.

For I decided to concentrate only on Jesus Christ and his death on the cross.
— I Corinthians 2:2 (NLT)

Most Christians don't see the need to not only go after Jesus — what He taught and said — but to go after the cross as well. There are three important things that Christians need to know. First, Jesus came to show us God's love and authority. He showed this to us on the cross. The cross shows you how you got loved. Second is the resurrection. We must know death can't stop the power of love. And third, the right hand of God shows you the authority or spiritual position of love, where you are seated with Christ in heavenly places. We can't go to the right hand of God to see how to love. Neither can we go to the cross and see how to be resurrected. Without the cross, it is impossible to see how to love like Jesus loved you and keep His commandments. Paul said, "For I determined not to know anything among you, save Jesus Christ, and him crucified."

The Message Bible makes it even clearer.

I deliberately kept it plain and simple: first Jesus and who he is; then Jesus and what he did — Jesus crucified.
— I Corinthians 2:2 (MSG)

You have to hear this over and over again so it can penetrate the way you have been thinking all these years and put the mind of Christ in you. The Bible doesn't teach you to have the mind of *God* — it teaches you to have the mind of *Christ*. When you get the mind of Christ, you have the mind of God, but you aren't supposed to jump to God and bypass Jesus. Now, what is the mind of Christ? What does that mean? People don't have a clue as to its meaning. The mind of Christ is having in your mind what Jesus Christ taught, what Jesus Christ said and what Jesus Christ did. The letters are to encourage you to live what Jesus taught, said and did. They point you to Jesus, but you have to know that Jesus is the one that originated all of this and the writers of the letters are following in His ministry, His doctrine and teachings. I can show you the teachings of Jesus in every letter. We have to get more focused on Jesus.

You must determine. The Lord isn't going to do this for you. If you start every day wanting to know the cross — Him crucified — it will change your life. It will make you more aware so you can walk in the light of the love of God. You will be full of joy hearing and doing this. When you walk in this you will have more joy than you have ever experienced before. I keep the joy of the Lord on me every day. I don't ever have a bad day. What? A day is going to come and whip Jesus - what He taught, said and did - And He defeated everything the devil's got; all the works of darkness? The Son of God was manifested to destroy his works! When I act just like Jesus, I've got to get the same blessings that He got. I never have bad days because I walk in the same victory Jesus had.

The most important thing to us as Christians is Jesus' commandments and teachings telling us how we are supposed to live. When Jesus is not the most important thing to you, then you don't know John 13:34 — you don't meditate on it day and night. I guarantee it; you've only walked in a small measure of this because that is the limit you have been led by your spirit. You haven't got revelation from the Word because you have not kept a picture of how to live this before you every day. A lot of people follow their spirit, but you only go so far when you follow your spirit and don't accompany it with what Jesus taught, said and did. When you have a foundation from the truth of Jesus Christ, there is no limit to where you can go.

Jesus did not ask you what you thought about people. He didn't ask for your opinion. He didn't ask how you felt. He doesn't care. He didn't come to care about what you thought. He came to tell you what God said and how to follow Him. So, when He gives commandments, they are not options. There are no "buts" in this. Jesus gave a new commandment. Why was it new? Because it could not be given until God's true character and authority had been revealed. In the Old Testament they understood portions of it; little pieces of it, but Jesus was the only picture of God and they didn't have Him. He was the perfect image of God. He was the pure likeness of everything God is, everything God says and everything God does. Nobody had ever seen that before.

O righteous Father, the world hath not known thee: but I have known thee, and these have known that thou hast sent me.
— John 17:25

Why is what Jesus is saying here right? Because He said it! That is an awesome revelation. "O Righteous Father!" Who is Jesus talking to? He's talking to the Father. "The world hath not known thee." What does that mean? In 1998 Jesus taught this to me. I looked up the word "world" in the Strong's Concordance and it's the same Greek word that is used in John 3:16 — "For God so loved the world." So He is talking about everybody that's ever been on the earth. Jesus said, "…the world hath not known thee: but I have known thee, and these have known that thou hast sent me." What can we get out of, "The world has not known thee but I have known thee"? You can use your brain right here — use just a little common sense. There was something that Jesus knew that nobody in the world ever knew. You can't get anything else out of that. That's very plain. You don't have to be a rocket scientist to figure that out. Jesus cannot lie so what He said was right. "The world hath not known thee, but I have known thee." What can we conclude from that? There was something that Jesus knew that no one else knew — no prophets, no kings, nobody down here on earth knew — except Jesus. Why do you think Paul said, "For I determined not to know any thing among you, save Jesus Christ, and him crucified"? Because he knew Jesus knew God; and if he didn't want to know Jesus and Him crucified more than anything else he would not get to know God. Now, what exactly was it that Jesus knew that the world did not know? Verse 26 tells us exactly what it was.

And I have declared unto them thy name, and will declare it: that the love wherewith thou hast loved me may be in them, and I in them.

— John 17:26

In the Strong's Concordance, that word "name" means "character and authority." There were two things that were not revealed in the law, that didn't come with Moses and no prophets ever knew. The first was how to love like Jesus. That's why we were given a new commandment. God had to send a picture down here of what love was so we would know how to love like Him. The second thing no one knew in the Old Testament was how to have authority over the devil. Nobody ruled the devil before Jesus. In the Old Testament God came down and whipped the devil for the Jews, but they never had authority over him.

Look what Jesus taught in Matthew 5.

Ye have heard that it hath been said, Thou shalt love thy neighbour, and hate thine enemy. But I say unto you, Love your enemies, bless them that curse you, do good to them that hate you, and pray for them which despitefully use you, and persecute you;
— *Matthew 5:43-44*

Moses told them to love their neighbor and hate their enemy because the flesh love can't love your enemy. It doesn't have the ability to love your enemy. But, Jesus said to them, "Love your enemies, bless them that curse you, do good to them that hate you, and pray for them which despitefully use you, and persecute you." Jesus has to be the picture on the cross of how to do that. Now, when you read that passage you still don't know how to do it. You know you haven't done well in that — loving your enemies and blessing those that curse you. You've just halfway done it and tried to do the best you could, but if you were looking at the cross and the picture of how you were loved, it would be easy. Jesus' yoke is easy. It's easy to love your enemies. God is never going to teach us to do something that is hard. Everything Jesus said is easy to do. Now, your flesh and intellect will tell you it's hard and get you in doubt and unbelief. You don't think it's hard when you need to be healed — you don't say, "I'm sick." Instead you believe, "Oh, no, by Jesus' stripes, I believe I'm healed." Most Christians can do that, but when it comes to love, you want to say it's hard. Jesus doesn't command us to do something that He has not given us the ability to do. Saying it's too hard to love is just as bad as saying you are sick. You must believe that what Jesus said for you to do, you can do, and that everything He said was true.

Jesus said, "I have declared unto them thy name — thy character and authority — and will declare it." This is the number one reason Jesus came. He did not come to the earth to die on the cross! Jesus is talking to God in this verse. Jesus' number one mission on earth was not to die on the cross, but to show us how much He loved God and

God loved Him — and through that love He went to the cross. He didn't go to the cross without love. He went to the cross through His obedience to the Father's love and to the Father loving Him. The Father told Jesus to come down to earth and die for us and He would raise Him up.

You can't treat people like Jesus did unless you die to self — and without that love you can't die. You have to give up your will if you are going to live this the way Jesus said to live it. If you don't, you are just trying to put on something like you are really doing it in front of people, but when someone does you wrong all that put-on you had is gone! The way you tell your love walk is by how you act when something goes wrong. That shows where you are in love. It's not how nice you are to people. Jehovah's Witnesses are nice to people. Muslims are nice to people. That doesn't reveal Jesus, just because someone is nice. They can't show the cross to anybody because they do not have the ability to love like God in Jesus; *but we do*. We have something no one else in the world has — authority over the devil and the ability to love just like God. No one else on earth has that. We have to walk in that more fully because this is what the world is waiting on. They want to see Jesus. When they see how you and I treat each other, they will see Jesus. They know no one in the world can do it. Now look at this verse in the Amplified Bible:

I have made Your Name known to them and revealed Your character and Your very Self, and I will continue to make [You] known, that the love which you have bestowed upon Me may be in them [felt in their hearts] and that I [Myself] may be in them.
— John 17:26 (AMP)

Why did Jesus need to reveal God's character and His very self? Because no one had ever known that. You have to know that Jesus revealed God's character His very self so that you don't have to look anywhere else for it. I'm not going to learn God's character from David or Job. I'm going to learn God's character from Jesus because Jesus said He is the only one that knows it. The Jews knew something about God's power, laws, what He said to do, and what He said not to do, but one thing God never revealed to them was how to love like

Him. They did not know how to love their enemies, they hated them. They could not rebuke the devil. Remember the word "name" means — character and authority.

The Message Bible says it this way:

Righteous Father, the world has never known you, but I have known you, and these disciples know that you sent me on this mission. I have made your very being known to them — who you are and what you do — and continue to make it known, so that your love for me might be in them exactly as I am in them.
— John 17:25-26 (MSG)

Most people say, "This is what I believe God did in the Old Testament." But you don't know what God did in the Old Testament until you learn the character of God in Jesus. You will blame God for things He didn't even do. Look at John 12:44.

Jesus cried and said, He that believeth on me, believeth not on me, but on him that sent me.
— John 12:44

In this passage Jesus cried. Jesus had tears in His eyes. You should really take note and listen when Jesus gets emotional. It really means something. Some of you might be thinking; when did they put that in the Bible? Well, it's been in there all along. When He first showed this to me I was astounded. God will keep showing you things in the Word, because you are still growing. If He ever stops, you have grown cold to Him and His Word. In John 12:44, Jesus said, "He that believeth on me, believeth not on me but on him that sent me." He is saying that when you believe on Him, you really aren't believing on Him because He never spoke anything of Himself. Jesus is the image of God, the character of God, the authority of God, the nature of God, the ways of God, the truth of God and the life of God. Jesus said, "When you believe on Me, you are really believing on Him who sent Me because I only say what I hear Him say and I only do what I see Him do. When you see Me you are really not seeing Me, you are seeing the One that sent Me."

Now look at Verse 45.

And he that seeth me seeth him that sent me.
                                           —John 12:45

Why is this true? Because Jesus said it! The more you say this, the stronger it will become in you; the less you say it, the weaker it will become in you. If you don't keep saying it you will lose it and you won't remember it anymore. The more you say it; it will stick with you, because faith comes by hearing and hearing by the word of God.

Let's look at the incident where the Scribes and Pharisees brought the woman who was caught in the very act of adultery to Jesus.

And the scribes and Pharisees brought unto him a woman taken in adultery; and when they had set her in the midst, they say unto him, Master, this woman was taken in adultery, in the very act. Now Moses in the law commanded us, that such should be stoned: but what sayest thou? This they said, tempting him, that they might have to accuse him. But Jesus stooped down, and with his finger wrote on the ground, as though he heard them not. So when they continued asking him, he lifted up himself, and said unto them, He that is without sin among you, let him first cast a stone at her. And again he stooped down, and wrote on the ground. And they which heard it, being convicted by their own conscience, went out one by one, beginning at the eldest, even unto the last: and Jesus was left alone, and the woman standing in the midst. When Jesus had lifted up himself, and saw none but the woman, he said unto her, Woman, where are those thine accusers? hath no man condemned thee? She said, No man, Lord. And Jesus said unto her, Neither do I condemn thee: go, and sin no more.
                                           —John 8:3-11

When they said she was caught in the act of adultery; they had to have seen it. When they brought her, it looks like they brought her to Jesus, but who did they really bring her to? They brought her to God. They brought her to who God is and what God does. Jesus was not going to say what He thought. God had to tell Jesus what He would say concerning this woman who was dead wrong. She was wrong; she was caught in the act of adultery, and was guilty. But they brought her to Love. What is God? Love. God is love. What is love? Don't say God, because where can you go with that? God is love, love is God, you lock yourself up in a vicious circle and don't even know where you are going with that statement. There is no revelation in that — it doesn't even say that in the Bible. The Bible says God is love, but it doesn't say love is God. Let me take you to revelation: God is love and love is Jesus on the cross. I have a picture now so I can see what *God is love* acts like without me thinking, having feelings, or figuring anything out. Jesus is it! End of story! He let her get away scott free. Why? Because He let you get away scott free. When someone does you wrong, the thought comes, "Are you going to let them do you like that?" Well, Jesus let you do Him like that, and He forgave you when you didn't deserve it. Why do you think *they* have to deserve it? You are not obeying His commandments if you don't forgive them when they don't deserve it.

When the Scribes and Pharisees wanted to kill the woman, what did they tell Jesus? "Now Moses in the law commanded us that such should be stoned..." Did the Law of Moses really say that? Yes, it did! Why? Because, there was no love in the Law of Moses. There was none of God's character, to bring you out; in the law. When they sinned, there was no forgiveness, there was no cross to bring them out. When they did wrong, they got what they deserved for doing wrong — death, because there was no life there to bring them out of death. Jesus said in Verse 7, "...he that is without sin among you, let him first cast a stone at her." The older people left because they had more sense than the younger people, but the younger finally left, too. They figured out that if the older folks were not going to kill her, they weren't going to either. The younger folks left last because they were the stubborn ones — they wanted to make sure that was really right. Now, who really told them, "You without sin cast the first stone?" God. What is God? Love. So who really told them that? Love. When you see this, you get a better picture of God.

In Verse 10, Jesus said, "...Woman, where are those thine accusers? Hath no man condemned thee?" Do you know what an accuser is? In the Book of Revelation it says the devil is the accuser of the brethren. He accuses the brethren day and night, but the devil is not omnipotent — he can't accuse everyone at the same time — he uses Christians to tell on folks. You are an accuser when you see someone who has done wrong — you know they did wrong, you saw them do wrong — and you go tell on them. When you do this, you are not acting like Jesus on the cross, you are working against God and acting just like the devil. You are not working *with* what God did for people on the cross, you are working *against* it. Jesus wants them to be free whether they get free or not. *You* must want people free whether they get free or not. If they don't repent, death will come to them, but don't have anything to do with their outcome because God didn't have anything to do with death coming to you. He brought life to you and wants you to act just like Jesus. If people don't act right, don't live right and won't repent, death will knock on their door. Don't have anything to do with them reaping death because Jesus didn't have anything to do with you getting death.

So even when people are wrong, you must want them to receive love, want them to get what you got when you were dead wrong and didn't deserve it. You must want them to get the same thing. If they don't receive it, it's not your fault. If the world doesn't get God's love, it's not His fault because He laid it out there. Lay out Jesus' love for people whether they receive it or not.

In Verse 11 Jesus said, "Neither do I condemn thee: go, and sin no more." That really wasn't Jesus talking there, it was God. What is God? God is love. Who was really telling her He didn't condemn her? God. Now I know God doesn't condemn. When you read the Old Testament it looks like God condemned a lot of folks, roasted some other folks, barbecued some folks, and drowned some more folks! But, do you get a picture of God like that in Jesus? No! If you believe Jesus is the way, the truth and the life; you have to look at what Jesus taught, said, and did to know God. The reason I know God doesn't condemn is because Jesus didn't condemn. If I don't see Jesus doing it, I don't have any business saying God will do it. You should not believe anything the Old Testament tells you about God that isn't in Jesus because if you do, you are saying the Bible is the way, the truth, and the life, and not Jesus who said He was! Jesus did not say *everybody* knew God, He said *He* did. The only God I know is the God in Jesus. This makes my faith work every day because I know how much He loved me on the cross and I never have any guilt, shame, or condemnation because none of that is from God; why - because it wasn't in Jesus. If Jesus didn't do it to me, God won't do it to me. What Jesus did to me on the cross, that's all God is ever going to do to me. If I don't accept the cross, I will get death. If I accept His love, I will get life.

Chapter 2

FOLLOWERS OF JESUS

There is no other life outside of Jesus Christ and Him crucified. You have to look to Him for everything. In every way you think, walk, talk and act, you have to look to Jesus, the author and finisher of your faith; because He has all the answers.

Whenever I read the epistles they have to preach Jesus to me. They can't give me anything except Jesus. Let's examine some of the statements Paul made in the epistles.

I can do all things through Christ which strengtheneth me.
— Philippians 4:13

Paul didn't say *you* could do all things through Christ which strengtheneth you. He said *he* could. That was *his* faith in Jesus Christ.

But my God shall supply all your need according to his riches in glory by Christ Jesus.
— Philippians 4:19

Paul didn't say *your* God was going to meet your need, he said *his* God was. That was *his* faith.

...but this one thing I do, forgetting those things which are behind...
— Philippians 3:13

Paul didn't say *you* were forgetting those things which are behind. He said *he* was. *You* can build from the foundation Paul had in Christ Jesus when you believe and extend your faith so that *you* can forget things which are behind in *your* life.

I press toward the mark for the prize of the high calling of God in Christ Jesus.

— *Philippians 3:14*

Paul didn't say *you* pressed toward the mark. He said *he* did. That's *his* faith. Your faith can only be inspired by the foundation Paul had in Jesus so that *you* can forget things which are behind and *you* can press toward the mark of the prize of the high calling of God in Christ Jesus for *your* life. You've got to find out about the faith that he had in Jesus so you know why he was talking like that instead of just reading what he is saying without the foundation of Jesus. Paul was looking at the cross that's why he forgot those things which were behind. He's looking at how he got loved in Jesus. That's how he knew he could do all things through Jesus.

Let's think about that for a minute. How can you do all things through Jesus which strengthens you? How can you? I hear people quote this verse all the time and they don't have a clue about what that means. It's just a quote from their heads without any insight or revelation as to what that verse means. What Paul meant was, "I can do all things through what Jesus taught, what Jesus said, and what Jesus did on the cross which will always bring me strength."

Now I have something to look at — I have a picture of Jesus. I have Jesus' teachings; I have Jesus' doctrine to look at to see what is going to bring me strength. You can repeat any of Paul's sayings, such as this statement,

I am crucified with Christ...

— *Galatians 2:20*

We can't just say that because Paul said it. Paul didn't say *you* were crucified with Christ, he said *he* was. That was *his* walk with Jesus. This is a perfect example why I followed Brother Kenneth Hagin. He spoke like that. I'm after his walk with Jesus, his love walk, his faith walk, his holiness walk. I have followed him for over 17 years. While he was alive I went and heard him three to five times every year; I never missed. What thrilled me about him was his love walk. He had testimonies about it. When you have been mistreated by others and you don't tell on them, that's walking in love. Preachers did him dead wrong, but he didn't go tell on them and get them in trouble. I love that! They got in trouble; but he didn't have anything to do with it because he knew love doesn't have anything to do with you getting in trouble.

Love will bring you out of trouble. Love will restore you and bring restoration to you. Really spiritual people are love people. Look what Paul said:

Brethren, if a man be overtaken in a fault, ye which are spiritual, restore such an one in the spirit of meekness; considering thyself, lest thou also be tempted.
— Galatians 6:1

Only the ones who are spiritual and are walking in love can restore those overtaken in a fault. How are you going to go to someone in the spirit of meekness, considering yourself? What are you going to consider? You are going to consider how Jesus loved you. That's all you can consider. Consider how Jesus did you and go act like that with the spirit of meekness that Jesus had. Jesus said He was meek and lowly in heart.

Come unto me, all ye that labour and are heavy laden, and I will give you rest. Take my yoke upon you, and learn of me; for I am meek and lowly in heart: and ye shall find rest unto your souls.
— Matthew 11:28-29

Most Christians don't live that. They act like Jesus didn't even say that. He told us to come to him when we labour and are heavy laden. We're not supposed to be depressed and worried — not if we listen to Jesus. Jesus also told us,

...In the world ye shall have tribulation: but be of good cheer; I have overcome the world.
— John 16:33

He has whipped every devil in hell and given us authority over all principalities and powers so that nothing shall by any means hurt us.

Behold, I give unto you power to tread on serpents and scorpions, and over all the power of the enemy: and nothing shall by any means hurt you.
— **Luke 10:19**

Jesus gave you power over *all* the power of the enemy — not just a little bit of it, not part of it, but *all* of it — and nothing shall be any means hurt you. I believe that! Why? Because Jesus said it! Your walk with Jesus is supposed to be easy, not complicated, not hard and rough. Things can come that are not easy but when you put Jesus on them — what He taught, said and did — the anointing on Jesus and His teachings will destroy every yoke and remove every burden giving rest to your brain. Jesus wants to give your brain rest! If you don't keep Jesus on top of your brain, it will go crazy. It will get off track.

Let's look at I Corinthians 2:2 again. In The New Living Translation it says,

For I decided to concentrate only on Jesus Christ and his death on the cross.
— **I Corinthians 2:2 (NLT)**

Paul said, "For I decided." God is not going to do this for you. You have to do it. You have to decide to concentrate only on Jesus Christ and His death on the cross. This has to be the number one thing in your life if He is going to reveal this kind of love to you. This kind of love doesn't pay anybody back — it doesn't get people. It doesn't go home from work or church and talk about people. It doesn't criticize people. Now, love will bring constructive criticism. Love will tell you that you are wrong, but it will tell you this in order to bring you out. Condemnation will tell you what you did wrong and lock you up. You are no good. You are nothing. Look what you did.

How many of you talk or have talked about a man or a woman in a political or high-ranking office who has done something wrong? I refuse to speak even one word against them. Why? Because I consider myself, "Now Robert Scales, look at all that you have done wrong and how you got loved; go give them that same love." I shut up. I remember I used to have a $200 to $500 a day crack habit. I used to rob banks, grocery stores and restaurants. I was a drug dealer, an alcoholic, a gambler and smoked cigarettes for 12 years. Jesus forgave me of all that! How in the world am I going to hold anything against anybody? He forgave me and cleansed me on June 30, 1988 at 10:35 p.m. At the Samaritan Drug Treatment Center on Shelby Avenue off North 6th I got on my knees and called on the name of the Lord Jesus. I surrendered my life to Him. I laid my life down and told Jesus that I was never going to serve the devil another day in my life. I surrendered everything. I told Jesus I was going to follow Him with all my heart, and since that day I have never followed the devil or practiced sin. I can't even relate to people who sin and don't repent. I can't understand it. I never practice sin. Not one day in over 21 years; since I've been saved and born again have I ever practiced sin. I don't even know what it's like to be wrong and not be sorry to God. I walk with God — I walk in fellowship with Him every day. I can't talk about people because of how I have grown in this.

I never talk about the sins of others. I can't throw any stones at them. I don't know why Christians haven't seen this yet. They have the nerve to give their opinion - "Why, isn't that a shame the way they did that." How do you know that you might not have done worse if you were in the same situation? You can't judge by the outward appearance. God is liable to give a man or woman mercy. You might think they deserve judgment, but He is the only one who knows the whole situation. They could get judged, but they might not. God is the only righteous judge. He didn't tell you to judge them. He told you to love them and pray for them.

Whenever I hear an evil report, I never open my mouth against those involved. I don't speak against anyone, instead I pray for them. That's why nothing in me is going to hurt — I hate pain! I don't get colds and flu. I just don't get them. Why? I don't believe in them. They don't come from heaven. Jesus didn't teach me that I'm supposed to have those things. He said He came that I might have life.

If they could find some Life Flu I would take that. I don't want Hong Kong, SARS or any of that stuff — none of that stuff touches me. I can hug people that have it and it will not get on me. You can't knock all this *blood of Jesus* off me, all this *anointing* off me and all this *greater is He that is in me than all the sickness and disease in the world* off me. I've been quoting Psalm 91 for years; no disease or plague will come nigh my dwelling and you mean to tell me SARS is going to knock down my faith in my Lord? No! I'm not scared of that stuff. It will not come near me or my family. It will fall down dead if it comes near us because I know how much God loves me. I know that Jesus loves me and I know that what His love did is greater than anything the devil can ever bring. I know He loves me because every time I get in trouble, every time I mess up; He delivers me, brings me out, loves me and He restores me.

This is how I learned a lot of this. When I did something wrong, I watched how the Holy Spirit dealt with me. He never condemned me or beat me up about it. He would wait a few days, then take me to the Word and chastise me. He would comfort me and draw me to Him, to the goodness of God, by telling me the Lord loved me. That's how you get folks set free — you tell them how much Jesus loves them. Love will bring conviction on them. It's the goodness of love that calls people to repentance, not how mad you are at them — that's not going to draw anyone.

My wife rejected me the first 12 years of our marriage. She was in bondage. She wasn't there for me for 12 solid years. She had an attitude. I'd ask her to do things. I'd say, "Honey, this is important for the ministry. I've got to get these letters mailed," and she'd forget to do it. I'd say, "Honey, that was important; I told you it was important. Why didn't you send them?" She'd say, "Get over it. I forgot to do it. Just get over it!" I would run straight to Jesus.

You are probably wondering what kept me in a marriage like that. I was not going to leave my son. I'm the only one that can raise him. I made a covenant with my son that I would never leave him like my dad left me. I was not leaving my child. I'm not judging your situation; don't get condemned because of my faith and commitment to God, but I refused to leave my son. One of two things had to happen: I was either going to get another woman to satisfy me or I was going to get to Jesus and let Him satisfy me. I chose Jesus and He kept me. He taught me how to love my wife despite how she acted. Do you know what kept peace in my home? Over 9 years of those 12 we never argued. She'd fuss, but I wouldn't — it takes two people to argue. Do you know what gave me victory at home? I worshipped God. You could be sick and walk in my house and get healed because the peace and glory of God were there — I worshiped, honored and glorified God every day.

I did everything Jesus told me to do. Don't get mad at me if you haven't lived like this. Jesus can't ask me to do anything that I won't do. He can't command me to do anything I won't live. He can't speak anything to me that I won't do. Whatever He says is, "Yes, Sir!" When He tells me to give, I say, "Yes, Sir, Lord, I'll do it — I'll do exactly what you told me."

He told me several years ago to give Rhema Bible Training Center a special one-time gift of $5,000. I said, "Yes, Sir, I'll do it!" Now, I did choke a little bit trying to get that out of my mouth. God is liable to tell you to do something that may make you swallow hard! I obeyed what the Lord told me to do. At that time I had been believing God for several new suits and didn't have the money to buy them. I prayed for everything. All I wear is alligator shoes and I prayed for every pair of them. They cost $700 a pair. Let me tell you something before you get mad because God has blessed me. I wore one pair of shoes and three suits for four years. I had no diamonds, no 14K gold watch and no diamond tie pin. My suits were tearing and ripping and I had deodorant stains in my underarms where I had dry-cleaned them so much. I lived in an apartment for 11 ½ years before God blessed us with a new home. I now drive a brand new Lexus; I get a new one ever two years. But, I want you to remember; I have served the Lord. I did not jump up to this. I have continued being faithful to God. I've been walking in love. I've been using my faith. I've been obedient to God and He has been giving me the desires of my heart. I didn't get this overnight. None of this happened in a few years — it was a process of time.

Every time I pray I see the Lord come through in everything. I am in love with Him and He is in love with me. If God can take an old ex- (whatever I used to be that I don't remember I used to be) if He can do this for me, then what in the world can He do for you?

In 1988 in a vision He told me to quit my job and follow Him. I quit that day. I was sold out to Jesus. He couldn't tell me to do anything that I wouldn't do. About the same time I remember going on The 700 Club with Pat Robertson. Pat was interviewing me and I told him what I used to do. I said, "I called on Jesus and I have not wanted to do any of that since." Pat said, "What? You just quit all that at once?" I said, "No, Pat Robertson, I didn't quit, I gave my life to Jesus and He set me free!"

That's what's wrong with people — they are *trying to stop* their habits. Quit trying to stop! Start obeying Jesus and your bondages will begin to leave. If you will start obeying Jesus and doing what He says in His Word, things will start leaving your life. You will quit being mean when you love like He loved. You won't have to try to quit being mean; just obey His commandments and you'll begin to be conformed to His image. Quit working so hard at it — just obey what Jesus says and you will never be the same.

The Lord blessed us so much. When He told me to quit my job and follow Him, people called me an infidel and they tore me down, but I knew I did what God told me to do. After I was on The 700 Club, a pastor called me and asked me to come to Indiana and preach for him. I was all ready to go, but I never received the plane ticket he told me he would send me. I didn't have any money back then; but the Lord Jesus said He wanted me to go. I knew a gambling, hustling man who never loaned anyone any money. I knew him when I was out on the streets before I got born again, and would you know the Lord told me to go to him. He told me to and tell him that He said to let me have the money to buy a plane ticket. So, I drove over there and went into his office. He asked, "What do you want?" I said, "God told me this morning to come over here and ask you to buy my plane ticket to go preach for Him." He said, "How much is it?" It shocked me!

I had been trying to reach that pastor and wasn't able to. He never answered his phone. When I arrived he said, "I'm so sorry. We made the reservation and somehow it must have gotten twisted up and never made it to Nashville."

They had no idea I almost didn't make it. They blessed me so much at that church. They put me in a presidential suite. They took me to the best restaurants and when I left they gave me a big honorarium — they really blessed me. I had only been saved a year! I cried for hours thanking the Lord; He had done that and put me in that kind of position. When I returned home I repaid the man his money and led him to the Lord. He said, "Man, I didn't look for you to come back." I said, "I gave you my word. God made me an honest man. I don't lie. I don't cheat people." I hate that! I haven't gambled, drank, cursed, robbed, or smoked in over 21 years and never will. I haven't had any desire to do those things. I hate that stuff, but I love the people who do those things so I can get Jesus to them and help them come out of their sin. If I hadn't gone to Indiana, I would have missed God. People told me before I went, "If the pastor had wanted you to come he would have sent you a ticket." I told them, "The Lord told me to go."

A lot of people don't think Jesus can tell you what to do; but He knows where the fish is with the gold in its mouth. He knows how to make your business turn flips and prosper. He knows how to bless your marriage and your home beyond what you could ever think. He knows how to make your bank account bigger than you ever thought it could be. He knows how to make your body well. He knows how to keep depression off you and keep you in peace and joy. To walk in this you must learn how to get to Him; make Him right in your life about everything.

Some people don't care anything about what the Lord says to them because it doesn't match what they think. One example of this is meddling in other people's business. A lot of Christians are nosy! Paul told the church at Thessalonica to mind their own business.

And that ye study to be quiet, and to do your own business, and to work with your own hands, as we commanded you;
— *I Thessalonians 4:11*

Do you know what it means to mind your own business? Quit meddling with other folks — quit meddling in their business. This scripture tells us to study to be quiet. That word "quiet" means mind your own business. Quit telling others what you think they ought to do. You have to grow up. Did you notice he didn't tell you to stop? He said study. You've got to study to quit meddling in other people's business. That's a biggie. It took me years to overcome that. It took a lot of study. We're just humanly nosy. People like talking and that runs you away from growing in love. It takes you away from love keeps you the way you are because you can't see the light. That's not what Jesus taught you to do. Stay out of other people's business.

Now, go back to I Corinthians 2:2 in The Message Bible — it puts a different twist on what Paul is saying.

I deliberately kept it plain and simple: first Jesus and who he is; then Jesus and what he did — Jesus crucified.
— *I Corinthians 2:2 (MSG)*

Saints, living the Christian life is supposed to be simple. Did you notice Paul did not say here that he was deliberately keeping it plain and simple first who God is or who the Holy Spirit is? Jesus never told me to follow God, He told me to follow Him. When I follow Him, I follow God. That's the way God made for us to follow Him, by following Jesus.

Jesus didn't tell me to know God, He told me to know Him. When I know Him, He introduces me to the Father and the Holy Spirit. The only way you can know when the Holy Spirit is really speaking to you is when you know the character of God that is in Jesus on the cross. This is how you know God the Father and the Holy Spirit, when you know Jesus and Him crucified. You get to know the Father, Son and Holy Spirit through Jesus. You don't get to go to God and try to know Him without Jesus; because Jesus didn't teach that. When people do this they might have some truth, but their understanding is cloudy. It's like what Brother Hagin said about prayer — people stick all kinds of prayer in one bag, shake it up, and throw it all out one way. But there are many different kinds of prayer. People have done the same thing with love, too.

Love is not a feeling! The Bible says nothing about love being a feeling. Love is Jesus on the cross, it's how He loved you — This is God. You have to keep it plain and simple. Paul didn't teach much about who Jesus is. You won't find much in the letters about who Jesus is. You can find in the letters what Jesus did, especially about the resurrection, but you are not going to find out who He is except in the Gospels.

In the Gospels Jesus said that He was the bread of life; He was the resurrection; He was the way, the truth and the life. You will never really know Him without going to the Gospels. This is where He told us who He was. Jesus never identified with flesh. He only identified with who He was in God. Look at what He said,

...Ye are from beneath; I am from above: ye are of this world; I am not of this world.
— *John 8:23*

In Colossians Paul taught us that our lives are hid with Christ in God and that we are to think on things above and not on things on this earth.

If ye then be risen with Christ, seek those things which are above, where Christ sitteth on the right hand of God. Set your affection on things above, not on things on the earth. For ye are dead, and your life is hid with Christ in God.
— *Colossians 3:1-3*

Many people are setting their affections on things on the earth and they are not walking in the love of God. They will be nice, they will do the best they can; but they can never act like the cross because the cross has no partiality in it. The wisdom of God that is from above is pure, gentle, easy to be entreated, without partiality and without hypocrisy. The wisdom that is from down here on earth is sensual and carnal — it takes sides. It identifies with its race.

But if ye have bitter envying and strife in your hearts, glory not, and lie not against the truth. This wisdom descendeth not from above, but is earthly, sensual, devilish. For where envying and strife is, there is confusion and every evil work. But the wisdom that is from above is first pure, then peaceable, gentle, and easy to be intreated, full of mercy and good fruits, without partiality, and without hypocrisy.
— James 3:14-17

When you become a member of the family of God, you lose your identity with your race and identify with the family of God in Christ Jesus. You should only identify with who you are in Christ, a new creature, not your flesh. Jesus said the flesh profits nothing.

It is the spirit that quickeneth; the flesh profiteth nothing: the words that I speak unto you, they are spirit, and they are life.
— John 6:63

Paul said we are not to know anyone anymore except through Jesus.

Wherefore henceforth know we no man after the flesh: yea, though we have known Christ after the flesh, yet now henceforth know we him no more.
— II Corinthians 5:16

Love cannot side. It is one way; Jesus on the cross. It can't be anything else. When you keep that one commandment of loving one another the way Jesus loved you, you lose sides. Jesus said He didn't come to make peace on the earth, He came with a sword. He came to set father against son and mother against daughter. Why? Because if the mother is not going to follow Jesus and the daughter is, then Jesus will rip them apart and send that daughter the way He wants her to go. He doesn't want her to follow her mother if she is going to take her away from Him.

If any man come to me, and hate not his father, and mother, and wife, and children, and brethren, and sisters, yea, and his own life also, he cannot be my disciple.

— Luke 14:26

The word "hate" in this scripture means "love less." If you don't love less your father, your mother, your wife, your sister, your brother, your race, your culture, your background, and even your own self; Jesus said out of His own mouth that you cannot be His disciple. Why? Because He came to teach you how to love like Him; and when you are in your feelings and siding with people, He can't teach you that. He can only teach you how to love like Him when you love Him more than anybody else. You love Him when you take His commandments, His teachings and His Words to heart and do what He says no matter what anybody thinks about you.

There is persecution coming when we walk in this. The reason we as Christians are not being persecuted is because the Church is not walking like we should. When we walk in Jesus' commandments, the world will hate us. The Church isn't walking in it yet, that's why they don't hate us. They hate love because they want to side. When you quit siding and love blacks as much as you love whites, they will not like that. My race — the black race — doesn't like it. People have been mean to me because I walk in this. They better not talk about whites when I am around. I will stand up in a heartbeat and say, "I love the white race as much as I love the black race." I have not gone to a lot of churches to preach because I got up and told a group of pastors that. I know I'm not supposed to go to their churches anyway because they aren't ready for this message. They want to stay in their skin color. Your skin is really not who you are. Your race is not who you are. It does not identify you. That's what man came up with and taught us all our lives so the devil could keep us divided, and when we come to Jesus the devil still wants us to be divided. In Christ you are a new man and a new woman. You're not flesh. You have a flesh that you have to put under and deal with, but that's not who you are. Until you see this, you won't love right. You will be afraid to love people because of the way people will think about you and treat you when you act like Jesus. I'm not.

One of the reasons I have gone so far in this walk is because when my wife used to be mean and ugly to me, I kept forgiving and forgetting how she was treating me. Thank God she is free now. She used to reject me I would get up early that morning to pray and forgive her and forget it. The next night I'd go back and try to be with her again because I couldn't remember that she had treated me like that. When you don't remember what people did, you can love like Jesus. If you keep remembering what people have done, you will become just like them; mean. If you hold anything against anybody, it will fester and grow and your love will be gone. Many times people just get over their hurts, shrugging them off, but they don't grow spiritually because they are not looking to Jesus and the cross. You have to have Jesus and the cross to walk in love.

How many times did I forgive my wife and forget what she had done? As many times as she needed to be forgiven. Did she repent? No! Did she ever tell me she was sorry? Maybe one time out of one hundred! Jesus didn't tell me to love others only if they love me back. He told me to love my enemies. That means they have done something wrong to you. That means they have despitefully used you and persecuted you. Jesus told me to pray for them. You can't pray for your enemies if you haven't done these three things: 1) love them; 2) bless them; and 3) do good to them. If you have not done these three things, you can't pray for them correctly. Your prayers will not be heard.

But I say unto you, Love your enemies, bless them that curse you, do good to them that hate you, and pray for them which despitefully use you, and persecute you;
— Matthew 5:44

God taught me to read love verses every day — morning and night — I still do. I miss maybe four or five days a year when traveling. I read them every day. I meditate on love scriptures every day.

Love endures long and is patient and kind; love never is envious nor boils over with jealousy, is not boastful or vainglorious, does not display itself haughtily. It is not conceited (arrogant and inflated with

pride); it is not rude (unmannerly) and does not act unbecomingly. Love (God's love in us) does not insist on its own rights or its own way, for it is not self-seeking; it is not touchy or fretful or resentful; it takes no account of the evil done to it [it pays no attention to a suffered wrong]. It does not rejoice at injustice and unrighteousness, but rejoices when right and truth prevail. Love bears up under anything and everything that comes, is ever ready to believe the best of every person, its hopes are fadeless under all circumstances, and it endures everything [without weakening]. Love never fails [never fades out or becomes obsolete or comes to an end]...
— *I Corinthians 13:4-8 (AMP)*

Because I have kept my tongue free from evil and my lips from guile; my home is so blessed — just like heaven.

Likewise, ye husbands, dwell with them according to knowledge, giving honour unto the wife, as unto the weaker vessel, and as being heirs together of the grace of life; that your prayers be not hindered. Finally, be ye all of one mind, having compassion one of another, love as brethren, be pitiful, be courteous: Not rendering evil for evil, or railing for railing: but contrariwise blessing; knowing that ye are thereunto called, that ye should inherit a blessing. For he that will love life, and see good days, let him refrain his tongue from evil, and his lips that they speak no guile: Let him eschew evil, and do good; let him seek peace, and ensue it. For the eyes of the Lord are over the righteous, and his ears are open unto their prayers: but the face of the Lord is against them that do evil. And who is he that will harm you, if ye be followers of that which is good? But and if ye suffer for righteousness' sake, happy are ye: and be not afraid of their terror, neither be troubled; But sanctify the Lord God in your hearts: and be ready always to give an answer to every man that asketh you a reason of the hope that is in you with meekness and fear: Having a good conscience; that, whereas they speak evil of you, as of evildoers, they may be ashamed that falsely accuse your good conversation in Christ. For it is better, if the will of God be so, that ye suffer for well doing, than for evil doing.
— *I Peter 3:7-17*

At this point we have been married 20 years and as I said earlier, we haven't argued in 18. My wife has been delivered — she fasted for seven days and got set free of the fear that was controlling her life. She is so free now that she loves on me every day — she just loves to give me love. It doesn't get on my nerves — I won't confess the lie that it does — but if it could bother me, it would. She's always rubbing me and touching me now. I wake up sometimes and go, "What's this?" She didn't do that for so many years I wasn't used to being touched in the midnight hour. I thought it was a snake or something that had gotten in our house. She would say, "It's just me. I love you, I'm for you and I'm with you." She never said that to me the first 12 years of our marriage.

I've been in full-time ministry all these years and God has always blessed me. I've never paid a bill late. I've never been behind on anything in the ministry or in my home. I never pay one penny of interest on any credit card. I've never begged people. I've never swindled people. I just get on my knees and talk to God about it. I've been under God's anointing and people just want to bless you when you are anointed. God puts it in people's hearts to bless you when you bring them something from heaven. They want to sow into your life. I have lived on this all these years. We've not had to come up with any gimmicks. We don't tell people to send us $1,000 so we'll send them a piece of cloth. That won't get the devil out of your house. We're not going to lie to you. Now, if you want to send us $1,000 that would be fine, but we aren't going to send you a cloth back. You can send us a prayer request or a cloth and we'll pray over it and send it back to you, but we aren't going to mislead you. You should give because you love the Lord, not because of some gimmick. I really want you to hear what Jesus says in John 17:25.

O righteous Father, the world hath not known thee: but I have known thee, and these have known that thou hast sent me.
— John 17:25

Who is the world? Everybody that has ever been born. Jesus said they did not know God. Why is this true? Because, Jesus said it. When the prophets of old spoke something by the Spirit of God, it happened. But when they talked about God's character, I don't know if they are right until I go to Jesus and find out. I can't take anyone's word for the character of God. Why? Because Jesus told me no one knew Him.

Here is what people have done. If you are 18 years or older, when somebody did something wrong you have probably said, "God will get them for that," but you never said, "Jesus will get them for that." You always looked to God to bring punishment to people; you never said Jesus was going to. Most of us have thought like this. Why? Because this is what we were taught growing up by people who didn't have this revelation; they taught us, "God will get you." We know Jesus won't get anybody. We wouldn't dare say that about Jesus, but people say God will all the time. Remember, Jesus said the only way to know God is through knowing Him.

If Jesus didn't get anybody, where do we get the picture or revelation that God does? Who taught you that? It wasn't the Holy Spirit. Church goers are mean when they are done wrong. They are nice until something goes wrong and then they turn into another person. Have you ever seen that in the church? People are so nice — they will do anything for you — but then they get offended with one little thing and they turn into Dr. Jekyll and Mr. Hyde. You don't even know who they are anymore!

Have you ever been so mad at something or someone that you could not forgive? You couldn't even pray about it because you were so mad. You probably even messed up the church because when a person gets bitter they always look for company. Bitterness never likes to be alone. It always looks for company. That's the truth. The Bible says it in Hebrews Chapter 12.

Looking diligently lest any man fail of the grace of God; lest any root of bitterness springing up trouble you, and hereby many be defiled.
— Hebrews 12:15

Look again at what Jesus said in John 17:25: "...the world hath not known thee: but I have known thee, and these have known that thou hast sent me." I have met so many Christians that don't believe that Jesus Christ is the only person who ever walked the earth who knew God, but it's true. Adam didn't even know God. He knew about Him. When God does something for you, you know about God. People take their personal experiences with God and think they know Him.

One day in our apartment a few miles from where we live now, I was on my knees praying, worshipping and talking with God. He told me there was a lady outside that had a flat tire and she was going to knock on my door and ask me to help her. He said, "Now, you go help her." I said, "Lord, I don't want to help her, I'm in here with You. I don't want to leave. I don't want to go out there and get dirty. I want to stay in here and praise You and talk to You and You talk to me." You know that doesn't go anywhere with God. When God tells you to do something, just shut up and do it! All that old yap yap doesn't go anywhere. God didn't even respond to my excuses. When the doorbell rang, I got up, answered it and said, 'Yeah, I know, you have a flat tire. The Lord told me and He wants me to come out and change it." She said, "How did you know I had a flat tire?" I said, "I was praying and the Lord told me before you rang the doorbell that you were getting ready to come." I went out and got all dirty; I even got my hands so dirty I had to get a manicure afterwards! You know, people don't want you to lay hands on them if your hands are all dirty! They want clean, holy hands! After I helped her she said, "You're the nicest man I've ever met. You're so kind; you always smile and help people here in the neighborhood. We never see you unhappy. How do you stay like that?" I said, "Jesus. I obey Him every day." The Lord had told me about her in prayer earlier. He said, "She just goes to church, she doesn't live for Me." So I knew she wouldn't get to experience what I had had told her. She didn't have the peace and joy that I had because she wasn't living for Him every day.

Sometimes when people hear me say "I do everything that Jesus says," they say, "Oh yeah, right." It's not my fault they are not mature and don't know how to walk in this power and strength every day. They need to get the right words in their mouth, stop speaking doubt and unbelief about love, and walk in the light of what God has given them. You really can have victory every single day. When the lady told me what a nice man I was she didn't know me, but she had affection for me now. Why? I did something for her and helped her. That's the way most Christians are in church. God has done something for them and they have these feelings and emotions for God; but according to the Bible the only way you can love God is to obey Jesus' commandments. People have taken their personal experiences with God and think they know Him. The Jews did not know God; they knew about Him. They knew they had a covenant with God. They knew if they called on God He would come down and whip their devils, unless they were in sin. They knew if they were in sin, God would let death come to them. You might say, "Pastor Scales, God won't do that!" But He did it to His own Son! What is God? Love. What is Love? Jesus on the cross. What did Love do when all our sins hit Jesus? He let death come to Jesus. Why? Because Love cannot bless what you do wrong. He couldn't bless us. He had to let death come to our sin and He is still like that today.

If you don't let Jesus — the love and forgiveness of God; your redemption — forgive and deliver you out of what you have done wrong; you will also end up reaping death. You must let Jesus reap death for you so you won't have to. Somebody has to pay the price for your sin. God will not let any sin go unpunished — no, not one. He can't be Love if He does. Love has to punish sin; letting the wages of sin be death. The way God punishes sin is by letting what He is not come to it. When God gets to be Himself, everything in His way gets whipped. When Israel obeyed God, who could whip them? When they disobeyed God, who could not whip them? Why? God wouldn't show up. You can go back through the entire Bible and see this. Whenever you see death, look for disobedience. When you see life, look for obedience. God doesn't show up in sin. That's why Jesus told the woman caught in the act of adultery, "Go and sin no more because I didn't come for you to keep doing this. I came to set you free from it, to show you the love of God, to deliver you out of this, not for you to keep doing it." People think God's love will get people. Did Jesus ever get anybody? Mankind as a whole really thinks that they are right and Jesus isn't. Job can't teach you who God is. He was coming progressively to the light — Jesus was the light. Job made statements like,

> *...the Lord gave, and the Lord hath taken away; blessed be the name of the Lord.*
>
> *— Job 1:21*

Jesus didn't teach that, Job did. Jesus said,

> *The thief cometh not, but for to steal, and to kill, and to destroy: I am come that they might have life, and that they might have it more abundantly.*
>
> *— John 10:10*

Job thought the Lord was into destroying. God doesn't steal from people. He's not a thief. He doesn't give and take. You can lose it all because you are in the devil's territory — he will steal it from you, destroy your life, take all your life savings away, and take you to bankruptcy, but not God! If you hang around God, you get blessed. If you don't hang around God, there's no telling what you are liable to get.

God loves you. When you really understand this, you will never want to leave God. Where would you go? Who would you call on to help you? Who would deliver you when you mess up, get in trouble and are out there with the devil? How can you leave God? How can you stay mad at somebody and get off God's turf? That's scary. Your faith won't work and you won't get answers to your prayers anymore. That ought to frighten us, but it doesn't frighten most Christians. It frightens me. Hold something against someone and displease my Master? No way!

When I got saved I prayed for two hours in English and two hours in tongues every day. I cried out to the Lord for hours — I prayed, "Don't let Satan take me back." I didn't know anything about the Bible. One day the Spirit of God or an angel put their fingers in my back and pushed me into the kitchen where there was a Bible on the table. I heard, "Come and read." I had watched soap operas for years; The Young and the Restless; All My Children and Days of our Lives were my favorites. You must have a serious devil in you to watch those! I'm telling you, it's not the Holy Spirit, so what spirit are you going to call it? I remember the day I got saved. I had been in a drug treatment center for two weeks and had missed a few episodes of The

Young and the Restless. I turned on the TV, trying to catch up on what Jack and them were doing. I was sitting there, watching, when I heard a voice — during those first few years Jesus talked to me just like I would talk to people. He said, "You are hurting Me when you watch that." I was only one day old in the Lord. I said, "Lord, I don't want to do that." I don't like doing things that hurt Him. When you really walk with Him, He can feel what you are doing wrong. He really does. It affects Him because He lives in you. He said to me, "Unplug the TV and come in here and read My Word so I can talk to you." That's how I learned He talks to you through the Bible. I unplugged the TV and never watched that program again — I had only watched ten minutes of it! Since I've been saved I have never listened to worldly music. I don't have any taste for it anymore; I used to love it.

I started reading in Genesis and when I finished it, Jesus told me to go to Matthew. I read Matthew through Revelation for 3 ½ years. Matthew through Revelation. Matthew through Revelation. I'd start to read Revelation and He'd say, "Read it and get out of there. Don't study this right now, get out of there." So I'd read Revelation and I wouldn't meddle with it. I wouldn't give it one thought. Here's what I did — some of you need to go back and do this — I read Jesus' teachings and the letters over and over again. I never read them to learn — I read them to do them. What a different Christian you will be if you do this. When I read something for the first time I would say, "I'll do that, Lord Jesus!" When Jesus said, "Love your enemies," I said, "I'll do it, Lord!" Many people, when they read the Scripture that says, "Love your enemies" they become afraid because they are not reading it to do it. The fact that somebody would be mean to them frightens them. They haven't made the decision to do what Jesus said; so when their test comes they don't do it! I made that decision! Jesus said if someone smacks you on one cheek, turn the other cheek.

And unto him that smiteth thee on the one cheek offer also the other...
— Luke 6:29

When I first read this verse I said, "I'll do it, Lord! You watch, Lord Jesus, when someone smacks me, you watch, Master, I'll put my hands behind my back and I'll give them the other side, just like you said." Everything I read I told Jesus, "I'll do it, Lord!" I couldn't wait to get in a test to show Him that I loved Him and I would do it. Sure enough, about four or five months later I got both of my jaws broken. A guy smacked me on one side of my face and broke my jaw. I said, "You forgot the other side." Then he balled up his fists and broke my other jaw. Then he pushed me down to the floor; choking me in a head lock trying to kill me! Blood was coming out of my ears and nose. I couldn't talk or move my face; I was in so much pain. I cried out inside for Jesus to help me and immediately an angel or the Holy Spirit made him stop. I didn't see them that time, but I knew they were there. I sat on the couch and cried. I was hurting. All I could remember was Jesus said to love them, bless them and forgive them. Then from my heart I cried, "Lord, I can't tell him I forgive him because I can't talk but I do and I won't ever hold that against him the rest of his life. I wish I could tell him, Lord Jesus." Immediately my whole face was healed and blood sucked back into my body. It was gone! It scared me.

Jesus said,

Judge not, and ye shall not be judged: condemn not, and ye shall not be condemned: forgive, and ye shall be forgiven:Give, and it shall be given unto you; good measure, pressed down, and shaken together, and running over, shall men give into your bosom. For with the same measure that ye mete withal it shall be measured to you again.
— Luke 6:37-38

Jesus said if you judge not, you will not be judged. If you don't condemn, you won't be condemned. If you forgive, you will be forgiven. If you give, it will be given to you, good measure, pressed down, shaken together and running over shall men give into your bosom.

You know, the man that was trying to kill me wanted to give me everything after that. I went immediately and told him I forgave him and I loved him and I would never hold that against him. I showed him the cross. When you act like that, those that have wronged you can't win. That kind of love never fails. Yet Christians don't see this. You can't lose in loving like Jesus. Even if people get away with what they've done, you will still win! Jesus will have to make sure you get way more back than what they stole. If you don't judge them, don't condemn them and forgive them; God has to step in and make it all back up to you because you have done it the way He said to do it, in love. He has to make sure you get back more than what you lost because you are doing it Jesus' way.

Most Christians have never believed that Jesus is right! Isn't that sad? We as the Body of Christ have missed out on so many blessings because when people were mean and ugly to us we didn't bless them. That's why the devil hardly bothers us because we are doing things his way. If we bless people, he hates it.

I remember we had a neighbor who was mean to my "adopted" son in the faith, Billy. I treat him just like I do my natural son. My neighbor used to curse Billy and called him all kinds of names. I was training Billy at the time, getting this message into him. When my neighbor started acting crazy he was ready to run. He started crying and was ready to run off and leave. I said, "No, no, come on back here, Son." Most believers act like this; they want to run away when someone does them wrong. They begin to ignore them and won't have anything to do with them. I said, "Billy, that's the devil, he's persecuting you. Stand up and take it! Put some love on him. Go act like Jesus to him. Stand up!" Billy opened his mouth and the Word started coming out. He said, "I love you mister and Jesus loves you, too." When Billy did that, the man got madder. He came over to me and said, "Your son doesn't listen to anybody but you." I said, "Glory to God! I'm so glad I trained him good not to listen to you!" Billy went and bought him a Home Depot gift card and we took some barbecued ribs to his house. One day he called the police on us and got a ticket put on Billy's car. He kept harassing us, but we kept blessing him. I went over there and gave him a hundred dollar bill. I went another time and gave him a fifty dollar bill. I did what the Lord told me to do.

Now my neighbor is so nice to us, he wants to help us do everything around the yard. Love never fails! Some Christians have not walked in love long enough to see it work like this. You have got to stay in faith that love never fails because sometimes when you are nice to people they get meaner. You have to stay in faith to love the same way you stay in faith believing for your healing when it hasn't manifested yet. You never say, "It doesn't work" when you are in faith believing for your healing. You must do love the same way. You have to stay with it; it will come to pass. Love never fails.

Look at John 17:25-26 again:

O righteous Father, the world hath not known thee: but I have known thee, and these have known that thou hast sent me. And I have declared unto them thy name, and will declare it: that the love wherewith thou hast loved me may be in them, and I in them.
— John 17:25-26

Jesus' purpose was to come and reveal the character of the Father and His authority to us through how He loved Jesus. Jesus came to show us the Fathers love and the perfect demonstration was the cross. When Jesus was on earth He showed God's love to the Jews because they were in covenant with God, but when He went to the cross He showed it to us; the whole world. I can learn from the entire Bible, but I follow Christ and Him crucified.

The reason the church doesn't have much power is because it isn't Christ-minded enough — it doesn't concentrate on what Jesus taught, what Jesus said, and what Jesus did on the cross. You must also understand that everything Jesus said is not for us; even though we can learn from everything He said. One example of this is when the Pharisees asked Jesus about divorce.

They say unto him, Why did Moses then command to give a writing of divorcement, and to put her away? He saith unto them, Moses because of the hardness of your hearts suffered you to put away your wives: but from the beginning it was not so. And I say unto you, Whosoever shall put away his wife, except it be for fornication, and shall marry another, committeth adultery: and whoso marrieth her which is put away doth commit adultery.

— *Matthew 19:7-9*

Everything Jesus said was true but Jesus wasn't talking to the church in these passages. Even though He wasn't talking to us, it is still true. Now, I can learn from what Jesus taught about divorce; that under the law there is no forgiveness. If you divorce and remarry, you are in adultery and the person you marry is in adultery, because there is no forgiveness. In this passage there was no cross. There was no love. When you take this teaching and give it to Christians who have been forgiven, you condemn them and lock them up. You bring them under the curse when Christ redeemed them from the curse of the law. When you bring the cross to the law, it changes it. The penalty for breaking the law is changed by the cross. You can get forgiveness today because we are not under the law. In the law you couldn't get forgiveness, but we are now under grace. When you get remarried now, after you have repented for the sin of divorce, you can't be in adultery anymore because God can't remember that you've ever been married. So if you have divorced and remarried tell your wife or husband, "You're my first, Baby. I haven't got any past!" The Son sets you free from your mess up!

You should never lie and say you have an "ex." If you have been forgiven you have no "ex," all you have is the baby or the honey you've got with you right now. When Jesus taught law, there was no forgiveness, so you had to be in adultery. You couldn't be forgiven. In Christ we have the mercy and kindness of God. We forgive murderers and drunks, but we don't want to forgive divorcees. Why don't you love them the same way Jesus loves? You must forgive them and forget they ever did anything wrong when you are walking in God's love. Even if it's your best friend's husband, get out of your feelings and emotions and quit siding and being partial. You are going to have to love your friend's husband if you are going to obey Jesus; even in the midst of having more affection for your friend. When you are in that "partiality/friend" feeling thing, you can't love and obey Jesus.

Look at Matthew 22:34-40.

But when the Pharisees had heard that he had put the Sadducees to silence, they were gathered together. Then one of them, which was a lawyer, asked him a question, tempting him, and saying, Master, which is the great commandment in the law? Jesus said unto him, Thou shalt love the Lord thy God with all thy heart, and with all thy soul, and with all thy mind. This is the first and great commandment. And the second is like unto it, Thou shalt love thy neighbour as thyself. On these two commandments hang all the law and the prophets.

— *Matthew 22:34-40*

Jesus wasn't teaching me to love God with all my heart, soul, and mind. Neither was He teaching me to love my neighbor as myself. Jesus was speaking to the Jews here. He said, "On these two commandments hang all the law and the prophets." In Verse 36, Jesus was answering a question He was asked by one of the Jews, "Master, which is the great commandment in the law?" In Christ you don't love your neighbor as yourself. Self, self, self. You don't have any self in Jesus. There isn't any *you* in Jesus. Your life is hid in Christ. In the Old Testament, they didn't have a picture of love to look at and see how to act. The best the law could tell them to do was to look at yourself and see how you would want to be treated and then love others like that. But in Christ, you don't look at yourself. You don't do the best you can. You don't ever get to bring you out. If you love your neighbor as yourself and you get in an argument with your spouse; when you leave the house, you will give people how you feel about you. That's not good! In Christ you don't get to bring you out. No matter how you feel or how you have been treated, you are to bring out how He loved you, and how He loved you isn't how others treat you. In Christ, your feelings and emotions never get to come out unless they are in line with Him.

A new commandment I give unto you, That ye love one another; as I have loved you...

— *John 13:34*

If you keep this commandment of loving one another the way Jesus loved you, you are loving God. We love Him in Jesus because He first loved us. We don't love Him with our heart, soul and mind, because in the law they didn't know how to love.

If a man say, I love God, and hateth his brother, he is a liar...
— I John 4:20

The way you love God in Jesus is how you love your brother, and that's obeying Jesus' commandment. Everything about God and the Holy Spirit is tied up in Jesus this is how you love. Christians haven't focused on that with their whole life. They have not had their undivided attention on what Jesus taught, said, and did — especially about love, faith, and hope. They haven't dwelt on Jesus enough. It's a shame to get full of the teachings about faith and not have much in the area of love. Love should be out in front; focused on first.

You show your love for God through your obedience to Jesus' teachings. When you keep Jesus' commandment; you love God and one another. It's the whole law. It's everything God is. Where? In what Jesus taught, said and did on the cross. When you keep that, you are keeping all the law of God you are required to keep. That's how you please God, by obeying everything that Jesus taught. When Jesus is answering a question, learn from the answer He gives, but when He gives a commandment, go do it.

And it came to pass, when the time was come that he should be received up, he stedfastly set his face to go to Jerusalem, And sent messengers before his face: and they went, and entered into a village of the Samaritans, to make ready for him. And they did not receive him, because his face was as though he would go to Jerusalem.
— Luke 9:51-53

Do you know who the Samaritans were? They were half breeds; Jews who had missed God. They had married foreign people with false beliefs and did not do what God said. They did not receive Jesus and James and John became very angry.

And when his disciples James and John saw this, they said, Lord, wilt thou that we command fire to come down from heaven, and consume them, even as Elias did?

—Luke 9:54

Let's burn them all up! Let's roast them! Come on, Jesus, you know Elijah did that.

But what did Jesus do? Who is in Jesus? God. A lot of people think this is Jesus' teaching, but it's not! He never taught anything of Himself. He never spoke anything of Himself. You don't get a picture of Jesus; you get a picture of the Father in Him.

But he turned, and rebuked them, and said, Ye know not what manner of spirit ye are of.

—Luke 9:55

A lot of people think like James and John. If Jesus were here on earth, He would say, "You don't know what kind of spirit you have." It's the wrong spirit. Why? Because you are trying to make God be something you think instead of letting Jesus teach you who God really is. You can't go back to the Old Testament and know God's character. If you did, how would you know God really did those things? You would have to believe whatever you thought.

You can't even know the Bible is true. You can believe it's true, but you can't know it's true. What would you stand on to know it's true? I'm talking about the character of God. How can you know that what the writers said about The Flood, Sodom and Gomorrah, Job and God hardening Pharaoh's heart were really done by God? Just by reading; you can't. The only way you can know the truth about God is for God to send you a picture down here on earth of His truth and character. Then you would have to go to that character and listen to what it had to say to see if God was like that or not. If the picture God sends you of truth doesn't teach you that; you don't have any business believing it.

I can know what truth is by the picture of truth that God sent me. I have no business having any other picture of truth because the picture of truth didn't tell me to run to anything else. Jesus Christ is right! What Jesus taught, said, and did is the only way you will know the character and authority of Almighty God. Everything else you know about God is wrong if it didn't come from Jesus. It's wrong! You need to read the Gospels, especially the book of John, three or four times and pray God will reveal His character to you through Jesus on the cross.

In Luke 9:54, when James and John asked Jesus if He wanted them to command fire to come down from heaven and consume the Samaritans who did not receive Him, Jesus rebuked them and said,

For the Son of man is not come to destroy men's lives, but to save them...
— Luke 9:56

Who was in the Son of man? God. What is God? Love. Love didn't come to destroy men's lives but to save them. Who said that? Jesus. Why is that right? Because, He said it.

In that hour Jesus rejoiced in spirit, and said, I thank thee, O Father, Lord of heaven and earth, that thou hast hid these things from the wise and prudent, and hast revealed them unto babes: even so, Father; for so it seemed good in thy sight.
— Luke 10:21

The word "prudent" in the Greek means intellect. God doesn't reveal anything to smart people who think they know Him. He will reveal things to smart people who recognize they don't know and want to know, but if you ever bring your brains to Jesus and try to use your smartness with Him, He will never show you anything about the truth. You will think you know it, but it will not work for you. Why? Because, Jesus said so.

When you follow Jesus you will get smart, "...and hast revealed (not you figured out) them unto babes." Do you know what a babe is? I've looked this word up and studied it. A babe is an infant. Mothers understand that infants can't do anything for themselves. They can't hold their heads up. They can't eat by themselves. They can't even turn over by themselves. An infant can't do anything for itself. These are the people that God reveals His truth to — infants; who totally depend on the Lord to reveal Himself to them. These are the only people who will get truth with power. Their attitude is, "Lord, I don't know, show me."

Trust in the Lord with all thine heart; and lean not unto thine own understanding. In all thy ways acknowledge him, and he shall direct thy paths.
— Proverbs 3:5-6

Let's turn that around. Don't trust in the Lord with all your heart, lean to what your brain says, don't rely on the Lord, and He won't direct your path! Be wise and prudent and He won't reveal anything to you.

You have to get this main revelation or I won't be able to take you any farther. Jesus said...

All things are delivered to me of my Father: and no man knoweth who the Son is, but the Father; and who the Father is, but the Son, and he to whom the Son will reveal him.
— Luke 10:22

How many things are delivered to Jesus from His Father? All things. What does that mean? Everything. What does God have left? Nothing! That's why we don't go after God — we must go after Jesus. God gave Jesus everything He is. There is no more God outside of Jesus. You don't have to wonder if there is. That's what a lot of people think; Jesus left some things out. They think there might be some validity to what they learned in the Old Testament growing up. I have three Chinese words for their validity — phooey, phooey, phooey! Jesus said, "All things are delivered to me of my Father." Then He said, "...and no man knoweth who the Son is, but the Father; and who the Father is, but the Son..." He said no man. Not David; not even Abraham! I have had preachers argue with me over this and say, "Oh, Abraham knew God!" No, Abraham knew something about faith; Abraham did not know what Jesus knew. The people in the Old Testament knew what God came down and did for them and revealed to them, but God never revealed this mystery of love to them. It was hidden from the foundation of the world until Jesus came. The mystery is Christ — how God loved you and me — in us, the hope of glory. It was Him.

...Christ in you, the hope of glory:
— Colossians 1:27

In Luke 10:22, Jesus said no man. Why does no man know who the Son is but the Father, and who the Father is but the Son? Because, Jesus said it. The only word italicized in Luke 10:22 is "him." It was added to this verse; but we know it is Jesus talking about God. You cannot have God revealed to you unless Jesus does it. Why? Because He said that He has to reveal Him to you. You cannot figure Him out from Sunday School or by listening to what your grandma taught you growing up. We love grandma; but she was wrong if she didn't tell you what Jesus said and what He did on the cross. You can't side with your feelings towards your family just because they were nice to you. I don't care what folks have done for you — you have to side with Jesus! People have sided with their family, their feelings, their race, or how somebody has done them, and not with Jesus. These people are not Disciples of Christ because they have followed their feelings and not Jesus' teachings.

And he turned him unto his disciples, and said privately, Blessed are the eyes which see the things that ye see:For I tell you, that many prophets and kings have desired to see those things which ye see, and have not seen them; and to hear those things which ye hear, and have not heard them.
— Luke 10:23-24

Why did He say many prophets and kings? Because everyone did not serve God so He didn't reveal to them that He was going to send Himself down here in a body — the Messiah, the Anointed One — and the government was going to be upon His shoulders and we would call Him Wonderful, Counselor, Mighty God, everlasting Father, Prince of Peace!

For unto us a child is born, unto us a son is given: and the government shall be upon his shoulder: and his name shall be called Wonderful, Counsellor, The mighty God, The everlasting Father, The Prince of Peace.
— Isaiah 9:6

God came down to earth. Jesus was not the Father — the Father was in heaven. Jesus was the image of the Father — what the Father does, what the Father says, how the Father acts, and who the Father is. Jesus was God's voice to us. He was God's love to us.

When Jesus was on the Mount of Transfiguration and Peter, James and John went with Him, the glory of God came out of Jesus, and Moses and Elijah appeared.

And after six days Jesus taketh Peter, James, and John his brother, and bringeth them up into an high mountain apart, And was transfigured before them: and his face did shine as the sun, and his raiment was white as the light. And behold, there appeared unto them Moses and Elias talking with him. Then answered Peter, and said unto Jesus, Lord, it is good for us to be here: if thou wilt, let us make here three tabernacles; one for thee, and one for Moses, and one for Elias.
— Matthew 17:1-4

Peter had the nerve to say, "Let's build a tabernacle for all three of you." This upset God! Why? Because, Peter was trying to bring Jesus down to their level.

While he yet spake, behold, a bright cloud overshadowed them: and behold a voice out of the cloud, which said, This is my beloved Son, in whom I am well pleased; hear ye him.
— Matthew 17:5

God left heaven and came down to earth in a cloud and said, "This is my beloved son, in whom I am well pleased; hear ye him." He didn't tell you to hear anybody else because Jesus had the truth. That doesn't mean you can't learn from Moses and others, but He didn't tell you to follow them. That's what's wrong with Christians. They have too much junk mixed in with the truth that they have. I have all Jesus — I don't have anything else. What Jesus taught, what Jesus said, what Jesus did; what Jesus taught, what Jesus said, what Jesus did; what Jesus taught, what Jesus said, what Jesus did. I live that every day. That's all I think about. I have so much peace it's incredible.

When things go wrong, it doesn't bother me even though I do get troubled sometimes. I've gone through some great oppression over the years during my walk with the Lord. People have done some of the meanest things to me and it troubled me because it didn't bother me. I got messed up because it didn't bother me. It didn't bother me because I had that shield around me. When you obey Jesus it puts a shield around you and nothing can penetrate it. It would have to hit your obedience to His love before it hit you because you are obeying what He said. When you are not obeying what He said, it will hit you and it hurts.

Again, in Luke 10:23-24, Jesus said, "...Blessed are the eyes which see the things that ye see: For I tell you, that many prophets and kings have desired to see those things which ye see and have not seen them ..." Why didn't they see them? Why didn't King David and Moses and great prophets of old see them? Because, God had not sent a picture for them to look at.

Verse 24 goes on to say, "...and to hear those things which ye hear, and have not heard them." They didn't hear them. Why? Because, God hadn't sent His Words made flesh yet. They couldn't hear who God really was until He sent a picture and a voice down here. This is plainly written in the Bible. You have to fight Jesus if you fight this!

These things have I spoken unto you in proverbs: but the time cometh, when I shall no more speak unto you in proverbs, but I shall shew you plainly of the Father.

— John 16:25

Why did Jesus need to show them plainly of the Father? Because, they didn't know the Father. The Jews didn't know Him. Jesus told them they did not know the Father, but He did because He came from Him. You can't talk like that unless you know it all. He really did! Why? Because, He said He did.

At that day ye shall ask in my name: and I say not unto you, that I will pray the Father for you: For the Father himself loveth you, because ye have loved me, and have believed that I came out from God.

— John 16:26-27

You must get this revelation — this is strong. Why does God love you? Read what Jesus said — don't think for yourself! God only loves people in Jesus on the cross. He doesn't love people anywhere else. If you don't get to Jesus, you can't experience this love. You will go to hell with Him still loving you and giving you a way not to go to hell. We have been taught that love is unconditional. But you have never read that in the Bible. Jesus never taught that. Now there is a measure of truth in that, but Christians have made that *the* truth. But it is not *the* truth because *The Truth* — Jesus — didn't say that!

Here is the truth. God loves the whole world unconditionally on the cross. His love is conditional when it comes to you and me because, if you do not accept Jesus, that love is not coming to you and doing anything for you. It might give you mercy to bring you to Him. When you get mercy it comes and helps you when you are dead wrong. Love will cause you to conquer and totally demolish what you are standing against. There is a big difference when you are walking in mercy and when you are walking in love. God's love on the cross will not do anything for people if they don't learn to act like it. He can't show you His love for you until you get to the cross. Look what Jesus said in John 14:21.

He that hath my commandments, and keepth them, he it is that loveth me: and he that loveth me shall be loved of my Father, and I will love him, and will manifest myself to him.
— *John 14:21*

Jesus said the only people that He was going to get to love are the people who obey Him. What does He mean by that? Doesn't Jesus love everybody? Yes — on the cross. He doesn't get to show everybody because they are not cooperating with Him. He is only getting to love the people who keep His commandments. The areas you obey Him in are the areas you get to see love. The areas you don't obey Him in, you see trouble. You don't see any victory in the areas you don't obey Him in. Then Jesus said, "I will manifest Myself to him." It's only the person that obeys Him that He reveals Himself to — how to act just like Him and how to win and overcome the world, just like He did. He shows you how to win over what people do to you, what people say about you, and every test and trial that you go through — He will show you how to come right out of it and win over it and have peace while you are in the midst of it, if you are doing what He said to do. That's how you love Jesus. That's why God will love you, because you are loving who God sent. You are seeing who God sent is the right way to God, and that makes God able to show you love because you believe Who He sent.

Watch Jesus say the same thing so you won't think I am making this up.

For the Father himself loveth you, because ye have loved me, and have believed that I came out from God.
— *John 16:27*

If you really believe that Jesus came out from God, why don't you believe every word He spoke, that it's from God? Why is it we aren't taking everything Jesus said to the church and doing it?

Look at Verse 28.

I came forth from the Father, and am come into the world: again, I leave the world, and go to the Father.
— *John 16:28*

What do you want Jesus to tell you? Look at what the disciples said in verses 29-30.

His disciples said unto him, Lo, now speakest thou plainly, and speakest no proverb. Now are we sure that thou knowest all things, and needest not that any man should ask thee: by this we believe that thou camest forth from God.
— *John 16:29-30*

The word "proverb" in Verse 29 means "parable." Jesus spoke a lot in parables and the revelation of the parables is found in the Letters written by the Apostles. Ninety percent of everything that Peter, Paul, James, and John taught in the letters can be found in the Gospels. I can show you what Jesus taught in the letters. The Apostles couldn't teach anything else.

Verse 30 is where God wants to get you. Look at what the disciples finally became sure of. They said, "Now are we sure that thou knowest all things." Are you sure that Jesus knows everything? If you are sure, then you can't go to the Old Testament to know God. If you do then you don't believe that Jesus knows everything — you are thinking they knew more than Jesus. You want to take the Old Testament word over the character Jesus told you was really God. The Old Testament really is true, but the writers miswrote some things, like "God committed" when they should have written "God permitted." If you just follow Jesus, you don't have to worry about any of that, because you have the truth.

Look at Verse 30 in the New Living Translation.

Now we understand that you know everything and don't need anyone to tell you anything.
— *John 16:30 (NLT)*

Have you ever gone to Jesus and told Him how somebody mistreated you? You really don't have to tell Him how they did you because He already knows. What did Jesus tell you to do? Go love them, go forgive them, go bless them, and go do good to them! There is no sense in trying to talk Him out of His Word. Remember in John 13:34 Jesus said, "A new commandment I give unto you, That ye love one another..." How? "...as I have loved you." No matter how you are treated, that verse says the same thing every day. It doesn't change because you were mistreated. People think the Bible has flipped and God has made a loophole for you to have some feelings and emotions, but He didn't. The Bible keeps saying the same thing no matter what you go through, no matter how anyone treats you. I don't care what they stole from you or what they did to you, Jesus keeps teaching the same thing every day and it never changes. I don't care how you feel or what you think, Jesus keeps saying, "Love them as I have loved you." And "Forgive when you stand praying." John 13:34 never changes. I don't care how you have been mistreated. Jesus doesn't change His Words because you went through something. Some people think that how they feel means something. They don't mean zip to God!

Aren't you glad that you can come and stand before God in Jesus as though you never sinned? I'm glad that God saved me and delivered me and brought me out of all my troubles. I'm going to act just like Jesus and love just like Jesus whether you do or not. People can accuse me of anything, and I'm going to forgive them, I'm going to bless them, I'm going to do good to them and pray for them. I will not get onto them for what they said about me because Jesus didn't tell me to do that.

I know this works. What Jesus taught works. You have to become sure that Jesus knows everything. Your spouse might make you so angry that you want to choke them. You might even want to hit them with a skillet, but the love of God will constrain you, if you have His Word in you. If not, they better duck.

The greatest force that's ever been on this earth lives down on the inside of us. But it doesn't do us any good until we get that nature that lives in us on the outside and start acting like it — the same way that

Jesus did us on the cross, when He loved us when we didn't deserve it. When you act like that, you whip the devil all over again. How Jesus whipped the devil is how you whip the devil — love like He loved and walk in authority. That's how you whip the devil. He forgave everybody and it defeated sin, darkness and everything you and I have ever done. If you don't act like that you give the devil place. He has no place when you walk in love.

When people don't walk in this, you have to learn to love them anyway. God disagreed with the whole world, but He came and loved us anyway. You have to learn how to love and disagree. Who did God agree with here on earth except Jesus? Nobody! A lot of people, in their own human thinking, think that when they disagree they are released from loving. They are in their own thinking. They think, "I'm not going to have anything to do with them anymore." You'd better be glad God didn't do you that way — you would be on His hit list forever!

Chapter 3

YOU MUST DECIDE

Jesus told me to know God after Him. I don't think it has been made clear as to how to know God — how to know God's character and authority. The only way is through Christ Jesus. Every time you see God in the Bible, you should be looking at Jesus on the cross. Every time you see God you should be thinking about His character and authority that was revealed in Christ Jesus. Every time I see God I am thinking about Jesus and how He loved me on the cross and that's my picture of God. You have to hear this over and over to get this in you — let it add to the truth and revelation you have already received from the Lord. This should be the foundation of your life — Jesus' teachings in the Gospels — What He was speaking to the church. As I said in the previous chapter, there were times when He was speaking to the Pharisees and Sadducees; the Jews and those under the Law of Moses — He wasn't talking to us (the church) in every place. The Scriptures where He was talking to us concerning love and the cross is supposed to be the foundation. The rest of the Word is to add to this foundation and never take us away from Jesus and His teachings. As a matter of fact, if anything takes us away from His teachings, it should bother us. This becomes clearer in Colossians 2:6. Many people misunderstand what I teach — they think I am saying that we are just to read the Gospels. No, you won't go very far if you just stayed in the Gospels. They should be the most important part of the Word of God that you live, but the Letters open up the Gospels. No one should ever take you away from the Lord Jesus — what He taught, said and did on the cross.

As ye have therefore received Christ Jesus the Lord, so walk ye in him:
— Colossians 2:6

On one of my evangelism trips I was praying and seeking the Lord in my hotel room, and the glory of the Lord fell at the desk and this scripture opened up to me. I had read this scripture hundreds of times, but this time it opened up to me. The Lord told me, "...so walk ye in Him." What does this mean, "so walk ye in him"? What did you receive when you made Jesus your Lord? I said, "Forgiveness!" This verse says that whatever you received, walk like it. If He didn't hold anything against you, walk like that. It's not hard. He didn't get you for what you did wrong, so walk like that. How He loved you, walk like that. When you received Jesus as Lord He touched you and gave you peace, so be a peacemaker. Walk like that.

I kept reading.

Rooted and built up in him...

— Colossians 2:7

Who is "him"? Jesus. Now how can you be rooted and built up in Jesus if He doesn't say anything to you? You have to go back and find out what Jesus taught, said, and did if you are going to be rooted and built up in Him.

...and stablished in the faith, as ye have been taught, abounding therein with thanksgiving. Beware lest any man spoil you through philosophy and vain deceit, after the tradition of men, after the rudiments of the world, and not after Christ.

— Colossians 2:7-8

I asked the Lord, "Who would I have to look at if you are teaching me not to let any man spoil me? Who is "any man"?" The Lord told me, "The most important person that you've got to be watchful for is not the preacher, it's you." People think too much when it comes to God. You've got to not let *you* spoil you through your own philosophy and what you think about the Bible and not making Jesus the truth.

Here is what Verse 8 says in the Amplified Version:

See to it that no one carries you off as spoil or makes you yourselves captive by his so-called philosophy and intellectualism and vain deceit (idle fancies and plain nonsense), following human tradition (men's ideas of the material rather than the spiritual world), just crude notions following the rudimentary and elemental teachings of the universe and disregarding [the teachings of] Christ (the Messiah).

— Colossians 2:8 (AMP)

Christians have figured out too much of the Bible in their heads and it is all wrong. They have a little truth to go with it, but they are really messed up because they can't really act like Jesus, especially when somebody does them wrong. They struggle with going through something and hate it when somebody does them wrong. When you really walk in the character of God, you aren't like that. You don't care what anybody does to you because the Greater One lives in you and you can't wait to bless them, love them, do good to them, and pray for them. The more you see this, the more you run to help folks. Most people in the church, when somebody does them wrong, they run *from* them — they don't want to help them. They don't want anything to do with them anymore. That's not Jesus. That's not how Jesus loved us. That's not what Jesus taught. He sure didn't say that, and He sure didn't do that on the cross. He ran to everybody that was dead wrong and loved them. Even while we were yet sinners He died for us. Then He told you and me to treat people the same way that He treated us, to love everybody the same way He loved us. He didn't say love them based on how you feel. He didn't say love people if you think well of them. No, He said love the way He loved you. You have to keep a picture in front of you every day — of the cross and how Jesus loved you. When you do this you will run to people and have compassion on them when they are wrong because you see that is how Jesus did you.

Many pastors, ministers and other people have been through divorces and everyone left them, like they were embarrassed to be around them. I have had ministers tell me, "Oh, no, I can't be seen with him. It will hurt my reputation." Reputation? Jesus didn't care about His reputation. He hung out with sinners. He didn't care about what anybody thought. You aren't walking in love when you are thinking like that. I have helped those people — I didn't care what people thought because I know that love is not a feeling. That's how God loved me in Jesus on the cross. I didn't care, I helped them. Yes, I know they were wrong and they missed God, but remember what Paul said in Galatians 6.

Brethren, if a man be overtaken in a fault, ye which are spiritual, restore such an one in the spirit of meekness; considering thyself, lest thou also be tempted.

— Galatians 6:1

When you walk in love you are in the restoration business because that is the business that God's in, helping people come out of what they did wrong. That's what the cross did — it helped all of us come out of what we were in. Now some people might not accept that love so you can't help them, but you still keep loving them and want to see them come out, whether they come out or not. God wants to see the whole world accept Jesus, whether they accept Him or not. He has made a way for them to come out, whether they come out or not. So when people are ugly and mistreat me and do me wrong — which not many folks do because I go where God tells me to go — I don't go tell other people. I'm not going to publish how people mistreat me. Even if people steal from me, I'm not going to tell on them. That's not love. Now, if someone comes and asks me about getting in a business deal with them, I will tell them, "No, don't, they are thieves." When the Lord tells you that somebody isn't right, that's love. He's not publishing what everybody has done and putting everybody's business out in the open for others to know. But, if you come and ask me about a particular person, then I am bound to love you and protect you from walking into a trap. If you don't ask me, you are going into the trap because I'm not going to tell you, unless God tells me to. I will not publish stuff on people. That's not love. Most Christians have never learned these things and they have been in church their whole life. I Corinthians 13 tells us to pay no attention to suffered wrongs, to take no account of evil done to us, and to believe the best of every person.

I have been going into prisons and jails for many years and some of the inmates are full of the devil and get offended. They hate me telling them the truth because it doesn't agree with what they think. Jesus isn't ever going to agree with any of us. He only agrees with God. Some of the inmates have been mean and have gone back and talked to the others about me and said false things about me. But, I would come back and Jesus would heal people right in front of them. One man was on dialysis and he asked, "Can God give me a new kidney?" I said yes and we prayed for him and he was taken off dialysis — he had a brand new kidney. They kicked me out of the prison — they sent me a letter and terminated me. They told me not to lay hands on anybody anymore because it caused an uproar. There were men in there that had been bitten by dogs and were in pain — God healed them, even removed the scars. Hundreds of people were coming, really to see the show — and the Lord loves to put on a show, to draw people in. So they told me not to lay hands on people. I cried and cried. I prayed, "Oh, Lord, what am I going to do? I can't lay hands on them." God was just so gentle and compassionate concerning my ignorance. He said, "I don't need your hands." That was a shock to me! I just knew He needed my hands. People sing that song, "The Lord needs our hands." No, He doesn't. I thought that, too. Then a special anointing came on me. The Lord said, "From now on you just point at them and tell them in My Name they are healed." I have brought that anointing into the church, but I received that anointing in the prison.

The next time I went to the prison I said to the people, "Now all you that are sick stand up." One man had a large tumor on his chest and another man had a neck brace on — he had been running from the police and gotten hurt. He was groaning the whole service. He moaned as he was getting up. I pointed to him and said, "In the name of the Lord Jesus of Nazareth, be healed!" He started swinging that neck brace around. The other man took his shirt off, his tumor had left — he showed all the men because they knew he had had it. God saved the State of Tennessee thousands of dollars. It would have cost that to get that tumor taken off. God took it off for free! There was another uproar and they terminated me again. They told me I had started a riot because so many men were signing up wanting to come to the services. A hundred men, just like that, would stand up, get born again, and give their lives to Jesus.

The Lord told me to go back in there and fight, so I returned and asked the Warden, "What do you have against Jesus?" He became furious with me for saying that — he was a Christian and a real dignified man.

I said, "Why can't men stand up and testify?" I knew it was the devil. He said, "I'm for that." He was a Methodist man. The chaplain almost fell out of his chair because he was the one that was fighting me. He wanted the gifts to stop operating. I just kept on working. Don't ever pay much attention to the devil. Pay more attention to God and Jesus Christ, the power of the Holy Spirit, and God's Word. When you pay too much attention to the devil, you are really off track. He's been defeated. He's been whipped. He's really not as big a thing or threat as you think he is. Jesus put him under.

We saw victory after victory. We walked on top of the devil every day, laughed at him, and made fun of him. I have been back in the prisons ever since. We aren't scared of him. We just tell him, "This is how it is going to be. This is what God said. This is how it is and there isn't anything you can do about it, but sit back and watch God bless us so much until we can hardly stand it and we have to go out and bless others." Do you know what the devil hates more than anything else on earth? Love. He hates love because love whipped him on the cross. God forgave all of us when Jesus died for us. That was the love of God. He hates that because it whipped him. That's why he doesn't like you and me to act just like that — to love one another the way Jesus loved us — because that will keep him whipped. He can't bring strife or division into the church when you love like Jesus. It renders him powerless when you love like Jesus loved. He can't destroy marriages, he can't tear up the children by getting them out there on drugs, alcohol or cigarettes; he can do none of that, when you love like Jesus. That one commandment contains any law that God would ever want to give. Just one commandment. The church as a whole has never focused on this. Most believers in churches all over the world can't stand somebody doing something wrong to them. Why? They have never grown in this. They have never grown in love.

Many Christians don't even regard Jesus' teachings in red. Even Paul said to follow him as he followed Christ.

Be ye followers of me, even as I also am of Christ.
—I Corinthians 11:1

How are you going to know how Paul followed Christ if you don't have a picture of Christ and the teachings of Christ to make sure Paul was following Him? Am I just supposed to take Paul's word for everything? How do I know that he's not going to get into error? If I have Jesus' teachings, I can tell you when the writers of the epistles missed it. Paul wasn't always right. He missed it in some things. Because of Jesus' teachings I can tell you when they were out of love, for instance when strife got into the camp concerning Mark, and when Peter was showing prejudice, refusing to eat with the gentile Christians — people like you and me. Here come the Jewish Christians and Peter got up and wouldn't even eat with them anymore. Paul had to rebuke him because Peter wasn't walking in love. He was in fear, just like people today who are afraid to love like Jesus because it brings persecution. That's why if you don't die to self you aren't going to really walk in love. Most Christians are deceived thinking they are in the love of God when they are really in their flesh love and feeling love — when they don't feel right anymore they don't love anymore. They aren't in the love of God because when you are in the love of God it doesn't matter how you feel. It doesn't matter what you think. It doesn't matter what others do to you when you are in the love of God. When anything happens to you and you let it matter, you aren't in the love of God.

Let's read Galatians 2:20.

I am crucified with Christ: nevertheless I live; yet not I, but Christ liveth in me: and the life which I now live in the flesh I live by the faith of the Son of God, who loved me, and gave himself for me.
— Galatians 2:20

What does "I am crucified with Christ" mean? Paul was identifying with the fact that he died with Jesus on the cross — with the death of Jesus. He is saying he died just like Jesus. You have to go back and identify that you have died with Jesus. Some Christians have to go back and have their funeral. They need to go back and die. Don't lose the revelation, knowledge, and truth that God has already given you, but go back and die so that more love can work through you.

Paul said, "I am crucified with Christ: nevertheless I live; yet not I..." Did you know that there are two of you? One of you is a spirit man, born of God, and the other you is a flesh man. Paul talked about this in Romans 7.

For I delight in the law of God after the inward man: But I see another law in my members, warring against the law of my mind, and bringing me into captivity to the law of sin which is in my members.
— *Romans 7:22-23*

The law in your members is always waging war against love. Your flesh doesn't like love. You hit me, I'll hit you. You don't like me, I don't like you. That's how our flesh feels. It doesn't like being nice and giving folks what they don't deserve, unless they are family members and you are operating out of your feelings. But, if they are not a family member, and they hate you, your flesh isn't going to love them because the love of God hasn't been shed abroad in your flesh — it's only in your spirit. That's why you have to work out your own salvation. You have to work out the love He put in you — live it out. God is not going to live holy for you. He told *you* to live holy. He's not going to walk in love for you. He told *you* to love. He told *you* to go act like Jesus. He's not going to do this for you. He told *you* to do it. God isn't going to forgive folks for you. He's already forgiven them. He told *you* to forgive them. He is telling us that we can act just like Him because we have the same grace and the same ability and power that was in Jesus. We can be perfect, or mature, just like God. Jesus told us we could in Matthew 5:48.

Be ye therefore perfect, even as your Father which is in heaven is perfect.
— *Matthew 5:48*

Why would Jesus say something like that if we couldn't do it? We can be just like God because He gives us the ability, the power, and the truth — Jesus is the appearance of truth — so we can be just like God. You've got to change the way you think and quit seeing Jesus as some idol that you can't be like. Start thinking, I can be just like Jesus, I can walk just like Him, I can love just like Him, I can walk in the Spirit just like Him, I can have power just like Him, I can raise the dead just like Him, I can heal the sick just like Him, I can cast out devils just like Him, and I can forgive just like Him. Quit seeing yourself as some little nothing because you are more than that. When God did a work in you in Jesus, He made you something.

Paul said, "I am crucified with Christ: nevertheless I live; yet not I, but Christ liveth in me." Now, how does Christ live in you? If we read the rest of the verse, it will tell us.

...and the life which I now live in the flesh I live by the faith of the Son of God, who loved me and gave himself for me.
— Galatians 2:20

This verse really opens up in the Amplified version.

I have been crucified with Christ [in Him I have shared His crucifixion]; it is no longer I who live, but Christ (the Messiah) lives in me; and the life I now live in the body I live by faith in (by adherence to and reliance on and complete trust in) the Son of God, Who loved me and gave Himself up for me.
— Galatians 2:20 (AMP)

Now look at this verse in the New Living Translation.

I myself no longer live, but Christ lives in me. So I live my life in this earthly body by trusting in the Son of God, who loved me and gave himself for me.
— Galatians 2:20 (NLT)

Paul had this revelation and we have to take this revelation that Paul had so we can follow Jesus, not Paul. Paul was talking to the people back in his day that were around him. Today, you have to follow your Pastor as he follows Christ. I tell the people that God has entrusted me with, "Now, you follow me as I follow Christ." As a Leader in the Body of Christ we have to tell people this and then have Jesus so strong in us that they have something to follow. When you tell people this, it makes you accountable. You can't act any kind of way. You can't act ugly, because they aren't going to follow that. "...and the life which I now live in the flesh I live by the faith of the Son of God, who loved me and gave himself for me." Paul said that's how he lives — by how Jesus loved him on the cross. That should be your faith. You should love one another by your faith in Jesus, how He loved you, and treat everybody else the same way. That's how Christ should live in us.

In John 17:25 you will see where Paul got this. You must see where Jesus taught it so you can see where Paul got it from.

O righteous Father, the world hath not known thee: but I have known thee, and these have known that thou hast sent me.
— John 17:25

Paul knew that the only way he was going to know God was when Jesus Christ showed him. Why? Because, Jesus said He was the only one that knew God. Jesus said, "The world hasn't known You, Father, but I have. I know you." That's why Paul said, "The life which I now live in the flesh I live by that faith that Jesus had, how He loved me and gave Himself for me." He knew that Jesus was the only one that knew the character and authority of God Almighty. The Jews in the Old Testament didn't know how to love like God and they didn't have authority over the devil. You've got to know that. Nobody else knew that, but Jesus. So there's no sense in you going back to the Old Testament to try to find this. You can go back there and learn some other things, but don't go back there for this. Most Christians have. They want to go back and take their philosophy — their brain and intellect — and read stories in the Old Testament that says God killed people. It does say that, but Jesus came along and said this:

...he that hath seen me hath seen the Father...
— John 14:9

Jesus is saying you can't know God without Him. How are you going to go back to the Old Testament and find out if God really did those things unless the Truth tells you and shows you the real picture of

God? If the Truth comes and doesn't kill or destroy, and tells you that He is the light of the world and you are to follow Him, how can you have a God that kills and destroys when the truth of Jesus doesn't teach you that? The Master — the only one who knew God — is not of this world. You are of this world. He came from the bosom of God. And you are going to tell the Word, who was in the beginning, Who became flesh and dwelt among us, what you think about God and not let Him tell you who God really is?

Jesus saith unto him, I am the way, the truth, and the life: no man cometh unto the Father, but by me.
— John 14:6

Jesus has appeared to me five times so far over the years: three times for my own personal life and two times for my ministry. He gave me a message in 1994 for my ministry and then appeared to me again in 1998 and gave me this message for my ministry. I never saw Jesus, but His voice came right from the ceiling and he would come and teach me. He told me, "Many of My people believe that I don't make people sick." I knew He was talking about most of the Rhema churches because they believe that. Then He said, "But, they don't have a foundation from My Word of My character. I am going to teach it to you and you are going to teach My people love." He told me there are only two places in the Bible where you can know the character of God. First, you can see God before Adam sinned, because God created everything good and gave man authority over everything on the earth. That's love. Love rules and dominates the devil and darkness because it is light. Then He said, "The other place is in Me." That's how I know it was Jesus. He came during a six-week period and I would lie in bed and wait on Him. I would ball up in a knot and close my eyes tight and He would manifest and start talking to me and I would talk to Him. He asked me one morning, "Can you quote John 14:6?" I interrupted Him like a child. I was so happy I could do something He asked. I said, "Jesus saith unto him, I am the way, the truth and the life: no man cometh unto the Father, but by me." And Jesus said, "Well said." I had never heard anyone talk like that! Then He made this astounding statement that boggled my brain. He said, "Many of My people believe that I am the only way to get to God." When He said that I replied, "That's what I believe. I mean, it says you are the only way to get to God." He said, "I am the only way to get to God but that's not all I said here. Now I am going to open my character up to you; how to know God."

If ye had known me, ye should have known my Father also: and from henceforth ye know him, and have seen him.
— *John 14:7*

The Lord began to teach me. I had read this verse hundreds of times before the visitation in 1998 and had never seen this. Not only is He the only way to get to God; He is the only way to *know* God. Now, why is Jesus the way, the truth, and the life? Because He said so! It's so simple. That's the only reason He is the way, the truth, and the life, because He said it. You can't go back and find out if Jesus was right. You can go check everybody else out, but you can't check Him out. You have to believe. I can check Job out, line him up with Jesus and see if he was right about God. I can check Moses out and see if he was right about God by lining him up with Jesus. I can check Peter, Paul, James, and John out and see if they were right. But you can't check Jesus out. He's right because He said it. Jesus said, "If ye had known me, ye should have known my Father also." Now, who is "me"? We have lived on Jesus' title too long. You are not your name. Your name is how others identify you. You are what you say and what you do. Do you know who Jesus is? He is what He says and what He does. That's who you are. You are mean, kind, nice, depressed, distressed, angry, bitter, etc. — you are what you say and do. That's you. Jesus is not His title. You can't follow His name if His name doesn't say anything or do anything. You can't follow Jesus Christ's name. Your children can't follow your name. They have to follow what your name represents. People have been trying to follow Jesus and don't even know what He said. So when Jesus said, "If you know me," He can't be saying, "If you know my name," because there wouldn't be anything to know. He would have to be saying, "If you know what I teach, what I say, what I represent, and how I do things." When you see that, you are looking at God. Jesus said, "If you know me — what I teach, what I say, what I do — you will know my Father also. From henceforth you know Him — know God — and have seen

Him." How would you know God and see God? Because you saw Jesus and you heard Jesus. Most Christians have never seen this, and they are always in their head thinking about what the Old Testament said, what was written about God, instead of Jesus who was the way, the truth, and the life. They have never believed Jesus like they should. It's sad. That's why they don't give mercy to people many times, because they don't see the mercy that they got.

But God commendeth his love toward us, in that, while we were yet sinners, Christ died for us.
— Romans 5:8

Jesus loved us with a great love, He was rich in mercy, and we should be rich in mercy, too.

Philip asked Jesus a question in John 14:8 that astounds me.

Philip saith unto him, Lord, shew us the Father, and it sufficeth us.
— John 14:8

Now, that's a dumb question to ask right after Jesus got through telling him! You could hear this ten times and maybe get it the eleventh time. They didn't get it when He first said it. It just depends on how much you are in love with Jesus as to how much you are going to get; and how much you believe that Jesus Christ was right and everybody else was wrong about God and God's character. I'm not against what the prophets said and that what they said was going to happen. I believe in the Bible from Genesis to Revelation. I just don't believe in following the whole Bible.

Then spake Jesus again unto them, saying, I am the light of the world: he that followeth me shall not walk in darkness, but shall have the light of life.
— John 8:12

Here is what I say to people: Show me in the Bible where it teaches you to follow it. You won't find any scriptures to that effect. Jesus taught me to follow Him — He didn't teach me to follow anything else. That's where people have messed up. You can learn from all the Word of God if it helps you follow Jesus, but I don't want anything from the Bible if it doesn't help me follow Him. If you aren't going to help me follow Jesus, I don't want it. I don't want any "God is going to kill me." That won't help me follow Jesus. He came that I might have life and have it more abundantly.

The thief cometh not, but for to steal, and to kill, and to destroy: I am come that they might have life, and that they might have it more abundantly.

— John 10:10

I don't want any killing. I'm not going to see my Father like that. I'm going to see Him from the cross — how Jesus loved me when I was wrong. I'm not going to see God paying me back because that isn't following Jesus. If you believe that, you aren't following Christ because Christ didn't teach that. You have to make a decision. Are you going to follow Job or Jesus? You can't follow them both. I can't accept what anybody else said about God — Job, Moses, Joshua, anybody — if it doesn't line up with what Jesus said about God. Jesus said He was the only One that knew God, He came from God, and when I see Him I see God. Jesus only spoke what God speaks. Jesus only did what God does. Jesus came to earth to reveal who God is. When you follow Jesus you can't follow anybody else — unless they are following Him.

Look how Jesus responded to Philip in John 14:9.

Jesus saith unto him, Have I been so long time with you, and yet hast thou not known me, Philip? He that hath seen me hath seen the Father; and how sayest thou then, Show us the Father?

— John 14:9

"Philip, He that hath seen me!" He couldn't have been talking about seeing His name. No, he was talking about seeing how He operated — seeing what He taught, said, and did. "He that hath seen me hath seen the Father; and how sayest thou then, Show us the Father?" He was saying, "You are looking at Him when you look at me."

Remember what we read in Colossians 2:8?

Beware lest any man spoil you through philosophy and vain deceit, after the tradition of men, after the rudiments of the world, and not after Christ.
— *Colossians 2:8*

Paul is saying don't let anyone spoil you about God and disregard Jesus' teachings. That's what He was teaching the church of Colossae — not to let anybody get you away from Jesus — what He taught, said, and did — because Jesus was the only one that knew God.

Let's look at John 17:25 again.

O righteous Father, the world hath not known thee: but I have known thee, and these have known that thou hast sent me.
And I have declared unto them thy name, and will declare it: that the love wherewith thou hast loved me may be in them, and I in them.
— *John 17:25-26*

The word "name" in verse 26 means "character and authority." It even says that in the Amplified Bible.

I have made Your Name known to them and revealed Your character and Your very Self, and I will continue to make [You] known, that the love which You have bestowed upon Me may be in them [felt in their hearts] and that I [Myself] may be in them.
— *John 17:26 (AMP)*

Jesus said He will declare it. What is He going to declare to us? "...that the love wherewith thou hast loved me may be in them." Do you know what Jesus came down here to transfer to us? God's love. And because of that love, that's what made Him die. He died because of how much God loved Him and how much He loved God. Now, what's going to make you die? When you see how much Jesus loves you, and how much you love Him, you will die to self. You will have the same crucifixion that He had. It takes faith in that love to die to self. It really does.

Let's read these verses again because I want to knock the devil upside his head.

Jesus cried and said, He that believeth on me, believeth not on me, but on him that sent me.
— John 12:44

What does that mean? When you really believe on the Lord Jesus Christ, you are believing on the character and authority of God. You aren't just believing on Jesus because Jesus was the image of God. Let me take this a little further. The Lord taught me why Jesus couldn't sin. Many people believe that Jesus could have sinned. But I know He couldn't. Now, if He didn't obey God, He could have sinned, but let me tell you what Jesus did that put Him in a position where He couldn't sin. He kept the Father's commandments and abided in His love. When you do that, every word you say has to happen. Jesus said He could do nothing of Himself. His faith in His Word, through His obedience, locked sin out of His life. Did you know that's how you and I are supposed to be? Most Christians are sin conscious. They say things like, "Well, you know, we are all going to mess up." But Jesus didn't teach us to talk like that. Jesus said when you see me, you see the Father. Most Christian's faith never reaches the level — when you see me, you see Jesus. They think they can't believe that because they aren't living it yet. But if you believe it, that's what will make you live it. You don't live it first and then believe it. You've got to believe it first, speak it, and then it conforms you to it. It was Jesus' faith that kept Him from ever sinning. Our faith can do the same thing. Now, your doubt could say, "Oh, no, no, no, we are all going to sin." But, where do you see Jesus teach that? When you don't make Jesus right, you are always going to think what you think and tell others how you feel about things. You are no more making Jesus Lord than the man in the moon. You have to make Jesus right in your life if you are going to move on in the power of God. You have to make Him right. I don't care what you think. There have been times when I didn't feel like I was like Jesus, and I didn't even act like I was like Jesus, but I never moved off my faith. We have been taught to do that with healing. We can feel like we are going to die and still say, "I believe that by His stripes I was healed." But we haven't used that in the area of love like we should. We have too much faith in our inabilities and not in the faith of the Son of God — how He loved us and gave Himself for us. How He loved us makes us more than conquerors. Did you know that the Bible says that you are *more* than a conqueror? Do you know why you are more than a conqueror? Look at Romans 8:37 and it will tell you.

Nay, in all these things we are more than conquerors through him that loved us.
— Romans 8:37

We are more than conquerors through Him that loved us. That's what makes you whip stuff. God's love makes you win — makes you more than a conqueror. It's through His love. That's why you can overcome sin, sickness, disease, and darkness, because of how He loved you. You can overcome any addiction. The more people see how they were loved and act like it, the more power of God they possess and walk in. The less love they walk in, the more they just talk and rely on their knowledge. They have learned, but it doesn't work for them because they don't walk in it.

Look again at what Jesus said in John 12:44.

Jesus cried and said, He that believeth on me, believeth not on me, but on him that sent me.
— John 12:44

What is Jesus really saying here? When you really believe on Him, you are believing on the true character of Almighty God and His authority. You aren't believing on Jesus alone, but on the One that sent Him.

Look at verse 45.

And he that seeth me seeth him that sent me.

— John 12:45

So when Jesus didn't condemn the woman caught in the act of adultery, that wasn't Jesus. When you see Jesus, who are you really seeing? God. What is God? Love. So what are you really seeing? The character of the Father, and His character didn't condemn the woman caught in adultery. You saw Jesus, but you were really seeing Who was in Jesus and Who sent Him. Who sent Him said, "Neither do I condemn you. Go and sin no more." So what can you learn from Jesus about God here? He didn't condemn her. You know He can't change, so whatever you see in Jesus is how God has always been and always will be. Jesus didn't come and change anything in the Old Testament. Who God was in the Old Testament is how Jesus is. You have to know that. What God did in Jesus He did before the foundation of the world. He didn't change in the Old Testament. Jesus came to bring you the whole light of God so you could know Him, see Him purely, and know how much He loves you. Then you are to give that love away to others. Many people accept that love on the cross — forgiveness — but they never act like it. They just take that love and say, "I accept that forgiveness," but never go give it to someone else. That's obedience — to act like it. Thank God they receive that forgiveness, even if they don't act like it. At least they aren't going to go to hell, but they won't get any rewards when they stand before Him. They could die early by not treating people right. God is not going to bless those that act ugly. He will let death come to their sin because God can't bless sin. That's why He doesn't want us to sin — He can't bless sin, He can't anoint it. He can only anoint Jesus — His way, His truth, His life. He can't anoint anything else.

God is a Spirit: and they that worship him must worship him in spirit and in truth.

— John 4:24

What is God? He's love. So what is "a Spirit" here? Love. You can get the knowledge of love and not have the spirit of love. A lot of people are walking in love from their intellect. They are not walking in the spirit of love because they have no power. You can be ever learning about the Bible and never come to the knowledge of the truth that was in Jesus, how He loved you, and acting just like it. That's when you have truth, when you can act just like Jesus. That's truth. When you talk just like Jesus, that's truth. There is nothing else that is truth outside of Jesus. It might be a fact, but it isn't truth. "God is a Spirit, and they that worship him must worship him in spirit and in truth." Look at what this Samaritan woman said in verse 25.

The woman saith unto him, I know that Messias cometh, which is called Christ: when he is come, he will tell us all things.
— John 4:25

Now how did this woman know that the Messiah was coming? Because, the prophets of old prophesied that He was coming. Moses prophesied He was coming. Abraham saw that He was coming. But they didn't know what He was going to say and do. They didn't understand it. Even when God told them some of the things He was going to do, they didn't understand it. This woman said, "…when he is come, he will tell us all things." The New Living Translation says,

The woman said, "I know the Messiah will come — the one who is called Christ. When he comes, he will explain everything to us."
— John 4:25 (NLT)

Some Christians don't believe this. You need to believe that Jesus came to explain everything about God. He came to tell us all things. Now look at Verse 26.

Jesus saith unto her, I that speak unto thee am he.
— John 4:26

Jesus was saying He was here to explain everything. "I'm here." And people go way back to Job to try to explain God! They go back to the flood and try to explain God! They go back to Sodom and Gomorrah and say, "Oh, yeah, I know what God did back then." But does it line up with Jesus, the one who came to explain everything? What if they had a Hebrew error in their translation. If you look back at many instances in the Old Testament they wrote "God committed" things when the correct translation should have been "God permitted." If you just believe who Jesus is, it will straighten you all the way up. Jesus can explain everything to you. You say, "Well, how do you know God didn't do that? How do you know God won't hurt people?" Because, Jesus didn't hurt people. How do I know God doesn't kill? Because, Jesus didn't kill anybody. How do I know God won't pay you back for what you've done wrong? Because, Jesus didn't pay you back for what you had done wrong. He forgave you. That's God.

I've heard preachers say, "Now God is love, but He's got another side — judgment!" Jesus didn't teach that. That's philosophy and intellect. No, God is love. He's love in the morning. He's love at the noon day. He's love in the midnight hour. He's love if you do good and He's love if you don't. He's love if you act right and love if you don't act right. God is not who He is because of you and me. God is who He is because of who He is, and He's love every day. He's Jesus every day. He's the same in Jesus yesterday, today and forever. I don't care how you act; you can't make God change or quit being who He is. All you are going to get for the wages of your sin is death. You aren't going to get God. If you get God you are going to get love, restoration, deliverance, peace, and forgiveness. If you get death you didn't get God because God is light and in Him is no darkness at all.

...God is light, and in him is no darkness at all.
— I John 1:5

There is no darkness in God. He could not bless the people in the Old Testament when they kept doing wrong. He could not show them His love when they kept doing what they wanted to do because His wrath stayed on them — the wrath of love. Do you know what His wrath is? It's when you don't let Him do anything about your situation. His wrath is; He doesn't show up. If He shows up, He's going to bring life. If you don't let Him work in your life, you will stay under the wrath where He doesn't show up and you are in darkness and death. But if you let God show up, He is going to bring life and that in abundance. If you aren't receiving life, then He isn't there. Whenever you go through trouble, if God shows up, you are coming out of your trouble. If He doesn't show up, you are going to stay in your trouble. When Israel obeyed God, He always showed up with a mighty arm. The battle was the Lord's — He fought their battles for them. But when they began to worship idols and doubted God, they stayed in the wilderness forty years. The serpents started biting them, but it wasn't God. He wasn't biting anyone. He delivered them out of Egypt. He blessed them with gold and silver. He promised them a land of milk and honey. God said, "I am going to prosper My people. I love My people. I'm going to bless My people." But they doubted God and they got in trouble because He couldn't bless their doubt. The serpents were there biting them and because God is love He gave Moses a rod to hold up and He could start healing them. That's my God!

When you see death, Jesus isn't there. Don't make God be death. He's not. That's why death is there. God didn't create evil. He doesn't have any evil in Him. There is no evil in God. You would have to have some evil to make some. You can't make anything you don't have. God can't be the devil, and the devil can't be God. God can't do bad and the devil can't do good. You can't be both of them.

Then said they unto him, Where is thy Father? Jesus answered, Ye neither know me, nor my Father: if ye had known me, ye should have known my Father also.
— John 8:19

These were people that had God's laws, but didn't know Him. Now if they had God's laws, but they didn't know God; can you see why the church is confused today because they have not made Jesus right? God has had to treat a lot of believers today like they were Jews — just be with them and never reveal His true self to them. You see, when you accept Jesus, you belong to the Lord, even if you don't act like it. You are His. He paid for you and He isn't going to let anyone pluck you out of His hand because He loves you too much. He is limited in how much He can show you His love and reveal Himself to you based on your obedience to Jesus' commandments. You determine how much of God you are going to know by how much you obey Jesus' commandments. You can't know God any other way.

Let's look at verse 19 again. Why did they neither know Jesus nor His Father? Because, Jesus said they didn't. What other proof can you have? You can't check Jesus out. You have to look at His works, and know that by His works God is with Him. "If ye had known me, ye should have known My Father also."

Now look at verses 20 and 21.

These words spake Jesus in the treasury, as he taught in the temple: and no man laid hands on him; for his hour was not yet come. Then said Jesus again unto them, I go my way, and ye shall seek me, and shall die in your sins: whither I go, ye cannot come.
— John 8:20-21

Is this condemnation? No! Jesus never condemned anybody. If I tell you you are going to hell unless you accept Jesus as Lord and Savior; I am not condemning you.

Any time I put love on the end of telling you that you are wrong, it isn't condemnation. If I say that someone is wrong for what they did, but we love them and are going to pray for them, believing God to bring them out, I am not condemning them. This is simply telling the truth, and giving them the cross and God's love to bring them out of what they are in. If you don't give people love to come out of what they are in, you are condemning them. Look what the Jews said.

Then said the Jews, Will he kill himself? Because he saith, Whither I go, ye cannot come.
— John 8:22

What were the Jews operating in? Their brains. Just like a lot of Christians today.

And he said unto them, Ye are from beneath; I am from above: ye are of this world; I am not of this world. I said therefore unto you, that ye shall die in your sins: for if ye believe not that I am he, ye shall die in your sins. Then said they unto him, Who art thou? And Jesus saith unto them, Even the same that I said unto you from the

beginning. I have many things to say and to judge of you: but he that sent me is true; and I speak to the world those things which I have heard of him.
—John 8:23-26

Jesus kept telling them the same thing, but they wouldn't listen. This is just like a lot of Christians today — they want to keep believing what they think about God instead of listening to Jesus.

Verse 27 astounds me.

They understood not that he spake to them of the Father.
—John 8:27

Do you know that many people don't understand this? They don't have a clue that Jesus is speaking to us about the Father.

Then said Jesus unto them, When ye have lifted up the Son of man, then shall ye know that I am he, and that I do nothing of myself; but as my Father hath taught me, I speak these things. And he that sent me is with me: the Father hath not left me alone; for I do always those things that please him.
—John 8:28-29

Whenever you look at Jesus you can't see Jesus because He said here, "I do nothing of myself." You can only see who He was imitating and Who He was looking and acting like. People have separated Jesus and God. They say, "God is going to punish you." Then when they talk about love, they say, "Jesus will love you." But really, when you see Jesus, that's all of God that you can ever know; God doesn't have anything else outside of Jesus. People will try to separate them, but Jesus never did anything of Himself. You can't see anybody but God in Jesus. Jesus said, "...and that I do nothing of myself; but as my Father hath taught me, I speak these things. And he that sent me is with me: the Father hath not left me alone; for I do always those things that please him." Jesus was in so much faith and obedience to His Father that He said, "...for I do always those things that please him." Most Christians don't talk like this. I do. I say every day, "I always do the things that Jesus does and I always obey the Lord." If I fail to do this, I run to the blood immediately to get forgiveness, but my faith never quits believing what I said. This is how you grow in this.

Let's continue reading in John 8.

As he spake these words, many believed on him. Then said Jesus to those Jews which believed on him, If ye continue in my word, then are ye my disciples indeed; And ye shall know the truth, and the truth shall make you free.
— John 8:30-32

Jesus didn't say in verse 31, "If you continue in the whole Bible." He said, "If ye continue in my word..." All God's Word is good, but when it comes to knowing God, you have to line it up with Jesus. Jesus was pointing everybody to His Words so you could know the truth. He never pointed you to anything else in the Bible to know the truth except Him.

The Amplified Bible breaks down verses 31 & 32 making it clearer.

So Jesus said to those Jews who had believed in Him, If you abide in My word [hold fast to My teachings and live in accordance with them], you are truly My disciples. And you will know the Truth, and the Truth will set you free.
— John 8:31-32 (AMP)

What makes you know the truth? You have to read verse 31 to get the answer. How will you know the truth? When you hold fast to Jesus' teachings and live in accordance with His Words — when you act just like Jesus. When you obey what He said, you will get to know what was operating in Him. Then when you know what was operating in Him, it makes you free. When did it make you free? When Jesus died on the cross! Until you start acting like it, it is not activated to work in your life. You can accept it without doing anything, but it won't work until you act just like Him. That's why we don't look like Jesus, because we aren't obeying His commandment to love others the way He loved us. That's why people don't know the truth about what the cross really did for the whole world. That's why we aren't winning the lost in this world like we should.

God, who at sundry times and in divers manners spake in time past unto the fathers by the prophets, Hath in these last days spoken unto us by his Son, whom he hath appointed heir of all things, by whom also he made the worlds;
— *Hebrews 1:1-2*

God did speak to the prophets in the Old Testament. He loved the Jews. He showed the Jews that He loved them, but they didn't know how to act like how they got loved. They didn't know how to transfer to others the way He loved them because He hadn't yet sent them a perfect picture of His love.

Who being the brightness of his glory, and the express image of his person, and upholding all things by the word of his power, when he had by himself purged our sins, sat down on the right hand of the Majesty on high:
— *Hebrews 1:3*

These verses are powerful in the Amplified Bible.

In many separate revelations [each of which set forth a portion of the Truth] and in different ways God spoke of old to [our] forefathers in and by the prophets,
— *Hebrews 1:1 (AMP)*

So what did they get in the Old Testament? Separate revelations, each of which set forth a portion of the truth. They didn't get all of it. Jesus was all of it.

[But] in the last of these days He has spoken to us in [the person of a] Son, Whom He appointed Heir and lawful Owner of all things, also by and through Whom He created the worlds and the reaches of space and the ages of time [He made, produced, built, operated, and arranged them in order].
— *Hebrews 1:2 (AMP)*

Who built this world and arranged it in order? God's Word. And His Word became flesh. That's Jesus. That's who built it — His Word. Jesus was what God said and what God did. That became flesh, so we could know God.

He is the sole expression of the glory of God [the Light-being, the out-raying or radiance of the divine], and He is the perfect imprint and very image of [God's] nature, upholding and maintaining and guiding and propelling the universe by His mighty word of power...
— Hebrews 1:3 (AMP)

Look at these verses in the New Living Translation.

Long ago God spoke many times and in many ways to our ancestors through the prophets. But now in these final days, he has spoken to us through his Son. God promised everything to the Son as an inheritance, and through the Son he made the universe and everything in it. The Son reflects God's own glory, and everything about him represents God exactly. He sustains the universe by the mighty power of his command...
— Hebrews 1:1-3 (NLT)

Everything about Jesus represents God exactly. There is no God outside of Jesus.

Chapter 4

THE LOVE OF GOD

God's love is not gooey. It's not an emotion. It's not a feeling. His love can affect your emotions and feelings, but your feelings and emotions are not the love of God. The love of God is how Jesus loved you on the cross; let His love affect your emotions. That way if your affections and emotions want to go another way when someone mistreats you, you won't follow; because it isn't the love of God.

People have made how they feel the love of God. They have made their emotions for people the love of God. When someone does something they don't like, all those feelings and emotions they had for that person disappear. I've lost feelings for my wife before. I was full of emotions and feelings for my wife one day, then the next day she would do something wrong and they would vanish. Disappear! Now, they are back! Have they ever left you? You cannot base your love for people on your experiences or feelings. If you could, whatever you felt about that person good or bad, you could say, "Well, that's the love of God." But, the love of God is not a feeling.

We need to see that love is Jesus. Everything Jesus did was God, and everything He said was God, because that's what Jesus said. When Philip asked Jesus to show them the Father, here was His reply:

Jesus saith unto him, Have I been so long time with you, and yet hast thou not known me, Philip? He that hath seen me hath seen the Father; and how sayest thou then, Show us the Father?
— John 14:9

Jesus also said He did nothing of Himself.

Then said Jesus unto them, When ye have lifted up the Son of man, then shall ye know that I am he, and that I do nothing of myself; but as my Father hath taught me, I speak these things.
— John 8:28

Jesus is the perfect picture of God. There is not another picture of God outside of Jesus. He is it.

One thing about God that many Christians don't understand is, He has a boot — He kicks. You might not think that this sounds like love, but it really is. God has a boot. Love kicks out. Remember in heaven when Lucifer rebelled against God? God's character — love — kicked Lucifer out of heaven. Love kicked Lucifer and a third of the angels out of heaven. After Adam sinned in the Garden of Eden, what did love do to protect him from the tree of life, so that Adam would not stay that way forever? Love kicked Adam and Eve out of the garden. What did love do in the temple when the people were selling things and making God's house a den of thieves and not a house of prayer? Love kicked them out. What did love do to the man who was in incest with his mother-in-law? This man wouldn't repent and deliberately continued living in sin in front of everybody. He had no remorse. What did love do to him? Loved kicked him out of the church.

What did love do when it came into your dead spirit? Love kicked out death! You see, love kicks out darkness. The more you walk in the love of God, the more darkness is kicked out of your life. It's not the more love you learn, it's the more love you live that kicks out more darkness. You have to understand this about Love.

Look at the example of the prodigal son in Luke 15.

And he said, A certain man had two sons: And the younger of them said to his father, Father, give me the portion of goods that falleth to me. And he divided unto them his living. And not many days after the younger son gathered all together, and took his journey into a far country, and there wasted his substance with riotous living.
And when he had spent all, there arose a mighty famine in that land; and he began to be in want. And he went and joined himself to a citizen of that country; and he sent him into his fields to feed swine. And he would fain have filled his belly with the husks that the swine did eat: and no man gave unto him. And when he came to himself, he said, How many hired servants of my father's have bread

enough and to spare, and I perish with hunger! I will arise and go to my father, and will say unto him, Father, I have sinned against heaven, and before thee. And am no more worthy to be called thy son: make me as one of thy hired servants. And he arose, and came to his father. But when he was yet a great way off, his father saw him, and had compassion, and ran and fell on his neck, and kissed him.
— *Luke 15:11-20*

There is something you have to understand about the Jews for this story to open up to you. Under the law, it was very bad for children who were disobedient. The Jews didn't whip their children much — they stoned them! That's why they didn't have prisons. They got rid of all the bad children. Some of you wouldn't be living today if you were under that law. So the people in the town knew how the son had disgraced his father. They knew. So they were waiting to kill him because he disgraced the family's name. He had disgraced his father. The father had to get to that boy before the townspeople did. He had to put his arms around him and embrace him so that death couldn't come to him. That's how our Father is to us. He's waiting to put His arms around people who have run from Him and have compassion on them.

And he arose, and came to his father. But when he was yet a great way off, his father saw him, and had compassion, and ran, and fell on his neck, and kissed him. And the son said unto him, Father, I have sinned against heaven, and in thy sight, and am no more worthy to be called thy son. But the father said to his servants, Bring forth the best robe, and put it on him; and put a ring on his hand, and shoes on his feet: And bring hither the fatted calf, and kill it; and let us eat, and be merry: For this my son was dead, and is alive again; he was lost, and is found. And they began to be merry.
— *Luke 15:20-24*

When the son left and went broke, his father wasn't even there. When you go out and start living wrong, God isn't even with you. When this son left to do his own thing, he got out from under his father's covenant, his father's blessings. All that misery he went through was not his father's love. He left his father's love. God gets blamed for people's mistakes. They say that God's love is doing that to them and it isn't. There is only one thing that God is going to give you and that is Jesus on the cross. He's not going to give you anything else.

For God so loved the world, that he gave his only begotten Son, that whosoever believeth in him should not perish, but have everlasting life.
—John 3:16

You have to meditate on this. "For God so loved the world..." That's all God is going to give you is Jesus on the cross. If He doesn't get to give you that, He doesn't get to give you anything. Now, you will get something, but it's not going to be from Him. People blame God for everything and it's just not so. He's not responsible for death. There is no death in God. He can't give you something He doesn't have.

This then is the message which we have heard of him, and declare unto you, that God is light, and in him is no darkness at all.
—I John 1:5

John said this is the message they heard from Jesus. God is light and there is no darkness in Him. God can't give you something He doesn't have. What God gave you was Jesus Christ and His love. He can't give you condemnation. Now, you can condemn yourself through your sin. You can stay under the condemnation of the sin of Adam, but you can't be condemned by God because there is no condemnation in Jesus. So, if there is no condemnation in Jesus, then there is none in God, because Jesus is God to us.

Another example of God's love is found in Luke 13:11-15.

And, behold, there was a woman which had a spirit of infirmity eighteen years, and was bowed together, and could in no wise lift up herself. And when Jesus saw her, he called her to him, and said unto her, Woman, thou art loosed from thine infirmity. And he laid his hands on her: and immediately she was made straight, and glorified God. And the ruler of the synagogue answered with indignation, because that Jesus had healed on the Sabbath day, and said unto the people, There are six days in which men ought to work: in them therefore come and be healed, and not on the Sabbath day. The Lord then answered him, and said, Thou hypocrite, doth not each one of you on the Sabbath loose his ox or his ass from the stall, and lead him away to watering?

— Luke 13:11-15

Notice the ruler of the synagogue said that people should not be healed on the Sabbath day, that there were six other days they could come and be healed! Imagine him telling God what to do, what day He should be healing folks! God doesn't ask you what you think about His will. No, He's going to do His will through those who will let Him, whether you like it or not! Jesus called him a hypocrite! Now, who was really calling him a hypocrite? God was calling that man a hypocrite! Jesus never spoke anything of Himself. A lot of people don't want to make God Jesus because they can't be mean anymore if they do. They can't talk about people anymore if they make God Jesus because Jesus never did them that way.

God said hypocrite. The Father was speaking through Jesus and calling that man a hypocrite. I have done that before. Shortly after I got saved I was playing basketball at the YMCA and this big old guy — I bet he weighed 400 lbs — stuck his elbow out and hit me, and boy did it hurt. The other team was supposed to be Christian men we were playing against. I walked right up to him and said, "Now look, I'm a born again Christian, filled with the Holy Spirit, and in love with Jesus, but don't hit me like that anymore." And he started cursing. When he started cursing, I said to him, "Only Christians come down here to the YMCA. You had to get a letter from your pastor to join." Then he started cursing about the church! And before I could think I said, "You big hypocrite! Christians don't act like that, you big hypocrite!" Then I went on and started playing again, and he didn't bother me anymore. The next week he came back — we were playing again — and he said, "Reverend Scales, I'm so sorry, I'm so ashamed. I couldn't sleep for two nights. I'm so glad you told me the truth. I was being a hypocrite. I go to church, but act another way down here playing basketball. I'm so glad you told me the truth because I would never have realized it if I hadn't heard it." I wasn't telling him he was a hypocrite to condemn him. I told him so he would know who he was and could repent and come out of it. When you tell people they aren't any good and leave them there, you are condemning them. But when you tell people their behavior isn't right and that they need to repent and come to Jesus, you are loving them. That's love. Anytime you are bringing them to Jesus, you are loving them. A lot of Christians are scared to tell people they are wrong because they are living in fear.

Now look at Verse 16:

And ought not this woman, being a daughter of Abraham, whom Satan hath bound, lo, these eighteen years, be loosed from this bond on the Sabbath day?
— Luke 13:16

Jesus brought a revelation here that no one else knew. Nobody in the Old Testament had a revelation about the devil. Jesus revealed here that Satan did the binding and Jesus did the loosing. Whenever you see binding, you know the devil is there. Whenever you see loosing, you know that love is there. God does not bind. As I stated previously, the devil can't do good and God can't do bad. God can't do evil. If God does evil, the Kingdom of God can't stand. If the devil ever tries to go and cast himself out, his kingdom can't stand. He has to be dirty, mean, dark, and evil every day. He never tells the truth. He will tell you something that is a fact to deceive you, to trick you into a lie, but he never tells the truth. Jesus said here that Satan had bound this woman for 18 years and she ought to be loosed. The character of Jesus here is revealing the character of God. Don't ever blame God for tying somebody up. Here is what Jesus told us to do:

But I say unto you, Love your enemies, bless them that curse you, do good to them that hate you, and pray for them which despitefully use you, and persecute you;
— Matthew 5:44

Jesus told us to love our enemies, bless them that curse us, do good to them that hate us, and pray for them that despitefully use us. Now why would the Lord tell us to do that if He's not going to do that? If God tells us not to pay anybody back, why would He pay somebody back?

People say, "Well, you know, Brother Scales, the scripture says, 'Vengeance is Mine, saith the Lord.'"

For we know him that hath said, Vengeance belongeth unto me, I will recompense, saith the Lord. And again, The Lord shall judge his people.
— Hebrews 10:30

But do you understand what vengeance is? God is the only One who can judge people correctly. He knows whether people are really wicked or whether they are just ignorant but sincere. He knows if the devil tripped them up. You don't know that, but He does. And so when vengeance comes, God will either give them mercy or He will let them get what they deserve. And He's the only one that can determine the vengeance on people because He knows the whole story about everybody.

You might have wanted some man to get knocked out because of the sin of adultery, but God could have seen that the man's wife wouldn't let him touch her for eight months - you judged the situation by an outward appearance because you don't understand love. We all know that adultery is wrong, there's no debate about that, but the penalty people try to give is wrong because it is not up to us to judge others it has to come from the Lord. Unless you are under my jurisdiction I'm not supposed to judge you. I'm not supposed to deal with you; I'm supposed to pray for you. I want to see Jesus and how He loved me on the cross - taking all sin away - coming to you when you don't deserve it. That's keeping Jesus' commandment. Jesus was teaching the Jews not to judge by the outward appearance.

Some people need to make some fresh commitments to the Lord; that they really want to love Jesus and obey His commandments and teachings. How do we love the Lord?

And there went great multitudes with him: and he turned, and said unto them, If any man come to me, and hate not his father, and mother, and wife, and children, and brethren, and sisters, yea, and his own life also, he cannot be my disciple.
— *Luke 14:25-26*

This scripture says that great multitudes went with him, so Jesus is talking to everybody here.

Let's look at another scripture that talks about being Jesus' disciples.

A new commandment I give unto you, That ye love one another; as I have loved you, that ye also love one another. By this shall all men know that ye are my disciples, if ye have love one to another.
— *John 13:34-35*

All men will know we are Jesus' disciples when they see our love one for another. Not by going to church. Not by tongues. Not by your gifts. Not by your talents. Not by how much money you have. Only by one thing — Christians are to be identified by the love we received from God in Jesus on the cross and giving that love to others. We aren't to be identified as Christians by anything else. Jesus didn't teach that. He said that when we act like Him, people are going to know that we follow Him. How we act demonstrates our walk with Jesus.

Remember Luke 14:26? Jesus said, "If any man come to me and hate not his father, and mother, and wife, and children, and brethren, and sisters, yea, and his own life also, he cannot be my disciple." This word "hate" means "love less." I read this scripture for years and just passed over it because it didn't sound right. It didn't make sense to me. But I found out that what Jesus is really teaching here is that you have to love everybody in this world less than Jesus — your father, your mother, your wife, your children, your brothers and sisters, everybody, it's got to include everybody — or you can't be His disciple. The definition of the word "disciple" taken from the Greek Lexicon means more than a New Testament pupil or learner. It means "an adherent who accepts the instruction given to him and makes it his rule of conduct." Jesus had disciples in the sense that they were His adherents who made His teachings the basis of their conduct. A true disciple doesn't have any other conduct. He's acting like Jesus, thinking like Jesus, talking like Jesus, quoting Jesus' words, and his mind stays on Jesus every day. That's a disciple of Jesus.

Jesus invites all those who come to Him to become His disciples. You are to take the instructions given to you and make them your rule of conduct. Love the way He loves you. You make that your rule of conduct, and have no other rule in your life. Now you can see why Jesus said in Luke 14:26 that you can't be His disciple if you don't love Jesus more than anybody else in the world. You will side with your family, your race, and even how you feel. And when you side with anybody against His teachings, He can't teach you how to act like Him. That's why a lot of people in the church aren't His disciples. They are church goers. A real disciple follows Jesus' teachings. He has no other way of living. I have no other way of living. I never do anything unless Jesus says to do it. I have no other life. I don't think any other way. I'm not afraid of what you might do to me. I don't even think like that. You aren't suspicious when you walk in love. Did you know you don't have to get rid of fear? If you walk in love like Jesus on the cross, it will cast out fear.

There is no fear in love; but perfect love casteth out fear: because fear hath torment. He that feareth is not made perfect in love.
—I John 4:18

People are trying to get rid of wrong lifestyles; but if they would just obey Jesus, they would start melting off. Your whole life will change if you just obey what Jesus taught, said, and did. The life that is in Him will begin to work in you. Love is the key. It makes faith work.

So then faith cometh by hearing, and hearing by the word of God.
—Romans 10:17

Look how this verse reads in the Amplified version.

So faith comes by hearing [what is told], and what is heard comes by the preaching [of the message that came from the lips] of Christ (the Messiah Himself).

— Romans 10:17 (AMP)

Faith comes by hearing what is told and what is heard comes from the lips of Christ the Messiah Himself — what Jesus said. Faith comes when you hear the message that comes from His lips. Jesus is the author and finisher of our faith so that's where you are going to get your faith in God — from Jesus.

Looking unto Jesus the author and finisher of our faith;...
— Hebrews 12:2

Faith works by love — faith comes by love when you hear how you were loved. Faith works when you see how Jesus loved you on the cross. It will make what you believe work. When you enter into prayer and worship Him because He loves you so much, you will be praying in faith. If you go into prayer with the attitude of how much He loves you, you can't doubt when you see love. Love doesn't let folks doubt. Love casts out fear. You can't doubt love because love will never let you down. There is no failing in love. When you see love, there is no way you are *not* going to make it because this love is only found in Jesus on the cross.

Look at Luke 14:26 again: "If any man come to me, and hate not his father, and mother, and wife, and children, and brethren, and sisters, yea, and his own life also, he cannot be my disciple." Why can't you be Jesus' disciple? Because, He said so; and the reason He can't make you a disciple is because your thinking is keeping you from Him. For example, you see things on the news and you start giving your opinions, you start saying what you think; you are a million miles away from love. You have no business meddling in our president's decisions. We have been praying for him to hear from God for months and you say, "Well, God is love and He's not going to send anybody to war and kill people." You don't know God. God told Saul in I Samuel 15:3 to kill all the Amalekites — the men, the women, the children, the babies, the animals, everything!

Now go and smite Amalek, and utterly destroy all that they have, and spare them not; but slay both man and woman, infant and suckling, ox and sheep, camel and ass.
— *I Samuel 15:3*

You say, "God is love, God wouldn't do that." God is love, but what you don't know about love is that love will let you reap what you sow. The Amalekites killed the Jew's children and babies when they came up out of Egypt — they hid in the bushes and killed them. In I Samuel 15:2, God said He remembered what Amalek did to Israel.

Thus saith the Lord of hosts, I remember that which Amalek did to Israel, how he laid wait for him in the way, when he came up from Egypt.
— *I Samuel 15:2*

God told Abraham that those that blessed him would be blessed and those that cursed him would be cursed!

And I will bless them that bless thee, and curse him that curseth thee: and in thee shall all families of the earth be blessed.
— *Genesis 12:3*

So what did God do? He would not bless their sin. He let them reap what they sowed. Death came to their sin, not God. If God had shown up, He would have forgiven them and delivered them. But, the true deliverance had not yet come back then because there was no Jesus. God had not yet shown a picture of how perfect His forgiveness was; that side of Him, the mystery of God. Do you know what the mystery of God is? It's the mystery of love. It's the mystery of who He is. It's how Jesus loved you. That's the mystery. Nobody had ever seen this kind of forgiveness. It blew the Jews' brains away when God showed the Gentiles love. They could hardly believe that God loved everybody. It was a shocker. Then the Holy Spirit fell on the Gentiles and it still took the Jews awhile to get a hold of the fact that God loved everybody. The mystery of Christ is how God loved you - the hope of realizing the glory. That's the mystery of God; and now that mystery has been revealed in Christ Jesus.

Even the mystery which hath been hid from ages and from generations, but now is made manifest to his saints: To whom God would make known what is the riches of the glory of this mystery among the Gentiles; which is Christ in you, the hope of glory:
— *Colossians 1:26-27*

That mystery has been revealed to the saints — how God loved us. It's been revealed, but the only way you are going to know this is by acting on it.

When we fenced in our back yard we bought a dog; he cost me almost $8,000. I've never seen a dog that expensive. Not only was he expensive, he chewed everything. He ate our dryer vents off, ate the steps, and chewed up just about everything in the garage. I had to build him a kennel on a concrete slab and put a wire fence around it. He also ate like a horse. One day I was training him in the front yard and he ran after this lady and her baby, scaring them. A broom was lying nearby and I picked it up running after him, hollered. I had told him not to go out there, but he ran anyway. You might ask, "You weren't going to hit him, were you?" Hard as I could! I was so mad! As I was running after him, I pulled a hamstring. Oh, it hurt! It was all I could do to get back to the house and up the steps. I was moaning. I lay in bed for three or four hours just moaning and groaning. I hurt if I moved a little bit; I even hurt if I was still. I finally got tired of that and said, "Alright, Lord, what's wrong?" Right then the Lord brought this revelation to me — it changed me and I pray it will change you. He said, "Love one another." He didn't add "dog" in there. I wouldn't dare treat a human being like I had treated my dog. When He said, "Love one another," I didn't think you had to love a dog like that. I didn't know. Then He told me, "Any area that you don't walk in love in, stops your growth in love." Once you walk in this, you can't stop. You can't ever be mad at anything. You have got to forgive everything that does you wrong. Let's say your car breaks down; you can't be mad at your car. You have got to forgive your car for breaking down or you will stop your growth in love. Any area that you don't walk in love in, you have stopped your growth in love. Jesus said you can't grow in love unless you continue in His words. I said, "Lord, I forgive Jett (my dog) and I won't ever hold anything against him the rest of my life." Immediately my leg quit hurting. All the pain went away. It was totally healed!

You see, when you walk in this you get corrected real fast. When Jesus is really your Lord and you are obeying Him, He has to make sure you stay on track with this. When you are not His disciple, He doesn't. You can act ugly every day if you want to. He won't say anything to you.

You have to know God on every side. Did you know it isn't a sin to be angry as long as you don't get out of love?

Be ye angry, and sin not: let not the sun go down upon your wrath:
— Ephesians 4:26

Every step out of love is sin. So if you get angry and you don't get out of love, you are all right. One time during His appearances to me in 1998 Jesus asked me, "Would you like to know what my anger is?" I balled up and said, "Yes, Lord Jesus, yes, Master." My entire Christian walk I thought His anger was like mine and it's not. The Lord Jesus said, "I get frustrated and irritated." I rebuked Him out of my ignorance saying, "No, no, no, You don't. You are perfect. You don't get like that." He replied very gently; because He knew I was ignorant, "Did you ever read in My Word where Israel provoked Me to anger?"

…they have provoked me to anger with their vanities…
— Deuteronomy 32:21

I replied, "Yes, Lord, I've read that." He said, "Let me show you what My anger is. My anger is when My people lock Me in a box where I can't move. It's when My people get in doubt and unbelief and keep Me from showing them My love, when they get death instead." God's anger is when Israel did not believe Him; He couldn't show them His love and He knew death was going to come to them in the wilderness. It angered Him when He didn't get any glory and the wrath of man came. It angers God when He can't be love to us. It angers Him when you lock His power up and He knows death is going to come to you instead of Him. That angers God. The godly anger that you should have is when you know somebody is not going to get the blessings, like when you see your children going the wrong way and you know they are going to get the wrong thing.

The anger of man is "be mean to people; don't have anything to do with people," but God's anger is when His people don't believe His Word. God, who is love, never gets glory when you go through tests and trials in your own strength. He doesn't get glory out of cancer or any other sickness. He doesn't get glory when you are broke. He doesn't get glory when you don't have a job. He doesn't get glory when you are depressed, or struggling, or when you have problems. He only gets glory when Jesus brings you out of these situations — when He heals you and delivers you, when His love is manifested to you. This is the *only time* God gets glory. He doesn't get any glory when He doesn't get to do anything for you. When Love doesn't get to do anything, God doesn't get any glory. So, when you forgive and forget how people treat you, God gets glory. When you walk in love like Jesus; you aren't suspicious or hold grudges, God gets glorified. You can tell when you grow in love because things will quit bothering you. Letting what other people do to me bother me isn't going to help me. God doesn't get any glory when you remember how someone bothered you. That's not His love. God isn't telling you to like the wrong people do to you. He's telling you to go to Jesus and act like Him toward them. I don't like a lot of things people do to me and say about me, but I still walk in love towards them. Look at John 15:9. This is how God loves you. He's not going to love you any other way.

As the Father hath loved me, so have I loved you: continue ye in my love. If ye keep my commandments, ye shall abide in my love; even as I have kept my Father's commandments, and abide in his love.
— John 15:9-10

Jesus never taught us to follow God. He never taught us to keep God's commandments. He never taught us to keep God's laws. Do you know what Jesus taught us? He taught us to obey *His* commandments, *His* teachings, *His* Words, *His* sayings. Jesus didn't say, "Continue ye in God's love." Why can't you continue in God's love? Because, you don't know God's love. The only "God's love" that you are to know is what Jesus showed you. The way Jesus loves you is the way God loves you. Your picture of God's love has to be Jesus; how He loved you and you continuing in that love. You should have no other kind of love than what Jesus showed you. Why? Because, He said so. To not believe this you would have to go to Walgreen's and buy yourself a whole bottle of ignorant pills and swallow the whole bottle up! You'd have to OD on ignorance to miss this.

Jesus didn't point you to God, He pointed you to Himself. Now, concerning prayer, He did point you to pray to the Father in Jesus' name:

And in that day ye shall ask me nothing. Verily, verily, I say unto you, Whatsoever ye shall ask the Father in my name, he will give it you.
— John 16:23

You aren't going to know how to pray to the Father unless Jesus' Words abide in you and you abide in Jesus. Only then can you go to the Father, ask what you will and it shall be done unto you. You still have to go to the Father through Christ. You aren't going to know that the Father loves you to be able to pray to the Father, to receive from the Father, until you see the love of Jesus and what He teaches about God. Then you can approach God to obtain mercy and grace to help you in a time of need.

Let us therefore come boldly unto the throne of grace, that we may obtain mercy, and find grace to help in time of need.
— Hebrews 4:16

Christians don't understand this because they are 90% law-minded — Moses-minded, ten commandments-minded, and just 10% Christ-minded. They have a little Christ in them, but very little, and it's choked out by law. It's choked out by people's thinking. It's choked out when you disagree with somebody and don't run to love.

Be ye therefore followers of God, as dear children And walk in love, as Christ also hath loved us, and hath given himself for us an offering and a sacrifice to God for a sweetsmelling savour.
— Ephesians 5:1-2

Verse 1 says to be followers of God. The New International Version says "imitators" instead of "followers", but it means the same thing. "Be imitators, or followers, of God, as dear children." Now if you stop right there, you will say, "Paul taught us to be followers of God." But you don't even know what God looks like. You don't even know what God acts like. Verse 2 tells you *how* to follow or imitate God. How do I follow God? How do I imitate God? "And walk in love, as Christ also hath loved us…" That's how I follow God. When I love like Jesus, I'm following and imitating God. Most Christians are trying to follow God without walking in His love — the way Jesus loved them. They are living in their thinking, their intellect, their reasonings, their theories, and their arguments — things that exalt themselves against the knowledge of God that was in Jesus.

Now, how do we know when something is exalting itself against the knowledge of God? Well, what is the knowledge of God? The knowledge of God is the teachings of Jesus Christ and what He did on the cross.

Casting down imaginations, and every high thing that exalteth itself against the knowledge of God, and bringing into captivity every thought to the obedience of Christ;
— II Corinthians 10:5

Look at this verse in the Amplified Bible:

[Inasmuch as we] refute arguments and theories and reasonings and every proud and lofty thing that sets itself up against the [true] knowledge of God; and we lead every thought and purpose away captive into the obedience of Christ (the Messiah, the Anointed One),
— II Corinthians 10:5 (AMP)

We are to cast down imaginations, arguments, theories, reasonings, and every high thing that exalts itself against the knowledge of God. How do you know when something is exalting itself against the knowledge of God? You bring it into captivity to the obedience of Christ Jesus. How are you going to bring those thoughts into captivity? How do you make something obey Jesus? You have to know what Jesus says and do it. You have to bring every thought that comes to your mind to the obedience of Jesus' teachings. When you say, "I can do all things through Christ," what is it that you can do? You can do everything that Jesus teaches, says, and does; this brings you strength. If all you have is, "I can do all things through Christ who strengthens me." I must ask you what is Christ? What did He say? What did He do that makes you able to do it? He told you that you could love like Him. This will bring you strength. Every time you obey Him, it brings you the strength of God Almighty, even when it doesn't look like you are going to win. Every time I loved my wife and forgave her for how she was doing me; she got meaner. It looked like it didn't work; but, I just kept reading the love verses every day. The revelation finally started getting in me that God doesn't change everybody because you walk in love. He changes you. Don't expect everybody to always just fall in line because you are lovey-dovey to them. That's not going to work. Walking in love keeps you from acting like them; it keeps you from getting under darkness and siding with the devil. Attacks come to make us leave love and get on the devil's turf where we can be tormented and defeated.

Look at Matthew 11:28-30. This is an astounding Scripture.

Come unto me, all ye that labour and are heavy laden, and I will give you rest. Take my yoke upon you, and learn of me; for I am meek and lowly in heart: and ye shall find rest unto your souls. For my yoke is easy, and my burden is light.
— Matthew 11:28-30

Most Christians think this is a fable. It's sad, but when most Christians have a problem, they don't go to Jesus. They don't believe His teachings. Whenever I don't have rest or get weary about anything, I haven't been with Jesus. Even though He is in me, He isn't manifesting Himself. I need to come to Him when I labor and am heavy laden. Why? So, He can give me rest. Now, how do I get this rest? Did Jesus say, "Take my yoke upon you and learn about the whole Bible?" No! He said, "Take my yoke upon you and learn of *me*." I'm not against *learning* from the whole Bible, but what Jesus was teaching here was how we are to stay in rest. He might send you to the Old Testament to get some scriptures from David by the Holy Spirit, but you are going to have to get your rest from Jesus. Why? Because, He said it. He said, "Learn of me." Why? Because, He is meek and lowly in heart. You will find rest to your soul because His yoke is easy and His burden is light. Most Christians have never developed in this. When they have problems they never go to Jesus. They tell their spouse, they tell their best friend, they tell their prayer partner and just blab off to everybody; telling them what so and so did and what's wrong with them. Don't misunderstand me; I'm not talking about testifying about a situation that glorifies God. I'm talking about people with problems. It's so sad; and they wonder why the Lord doesn't do much in their lives. They don't go to Him. I never run to anybody but Jesus. I had to teach my wife this. I told her to stop telling me what was wrong with everybody on her job. I didn't want to hear it. I would say, "Don't come home telling me how ugly they are. You should have prayed for them while you were at work. You ought to bless them and have something good to say about them when you come home. Don't come home filling my ears up with garbage about what people have done to you." When you walk in this, you are going to get persecuted. People think you're being mean when all you are really trying to do is obey Jesus. You will get persecuted from people who are close to you, especially family members, because they don't like love. They don't understand it and they don't like it because it doesn't side with them. Love sides with God; it doesn't side with anybody else. You must learn to run to Jesus. Why? To get your rest! Every time I go to Jesus, I get His rest. I follow His teachings. I obey Him.

Again, how does God love me? The way Jesus loved me. Remember what, John 15:9 says, "As the Father hath loved me, so have I loved you. Continue ye in my love." Who does Jesus always point you to?

Himself — His teachings, His sayings, and the way He does things. That is God; and that is the only God you ought to know.

I want to show you how you can know if you know Him. The Scriptures tell you whether you love God or not. It's not because you say you know Him. You have to do what the Scriptures say to do if you want to know God.

Beloved, let us love one another: for love is of God; and every one that loveth is born of God, and knoweth God.
— I John 4:7

Some people don't like this because it doesn't agree with the way they think. They become negative and start criticizing the teachings of Jesus. Look at what II John 9 says.

Whosoever transgresseth, and abideth not in the doctrine of Christ, hath not God. He that abideth in the doctrine of Christ, he hath both the Father and the Son.
— II John 9

Now let's look at this verse in the New Living Translation.

For if you wander beyond the teaching of Christ, you will not have fellowship with God. But if you continue in the teaching of Christ, you will have fellowship with both the Father and the Son.
— II John 9 (NLT)

John is not saying that you have to believe the Gospels only. He's saying that the Gospels have to be the foundation of the truth in your life. The Epistles and the Old Testament are to add to this truth. Nothing is to say it is right over Jesus. Nothing!

Let's look at this verse in the Amplified Bible.

Anyone who runs on ahead [of God] and does not abide in the doctrine of Christ [who is not content with what He taught] does not have God; but he who continues to live in the doctrine (teaching) of

Christ [does have God], he has both the Father and the Son.
— II John 9 (AMP)

Without the Son, you don't have God. Let me say that again. Without the Son, there is no God.

Look at I John 4:7 again.

Beloved, let us love one another: for love is of God; and every one that loveth is born of God, and knoweth God. He that loveth not knoweth not God; for God is love.
—I John 4:7-8

What are they really born of? Love. So when you are born of God, you are really born of love. It goes on, "...and knoweth God." What do you really know? You know love. Now, here is my question: How do you know love? This verse will tell you, "...and every one that loveth." Loveth? How do you loveth? Let me break it down. Everyone that loves — if you aren't bringing Jesus and Him crucified here, this is not going to make sense to you. You are not going to know what love means. Everyone that loves like Jesus on the cross. Everyone that loves how? As He has loved you. You have to put Jesus' commandment there. Everyone that loves like Jesus. When they do this there are two things you can tell about that person. You know they are born of love and you know they know God. What is it they really know? They know Love. Now, here is another question to you: How do you know love? It's when you act like it, not when you receive it. I don't care what God has done for you. I don't care how God has blessed you. It doesn't make you know Him. It makes you know *about* Him. You can only know God when you obey love and act just like Him.

Jesus taught the same thing in John 8:31-32

Then said Jesus to those Jews which believed on him, If ye continue in my word, then are ye my disciples indeed; And ye shall know the truth, and the truth shall make you free.
— John 8:31-32

Jesus said if you continue in His words you will know the truth. When you don't love, you don't know the true God. Even though the true God may have shown you a lot of love, answered your prayers, given you comfort, and come through for you in the midnight hour, it does not mean you know Him. You don't know Him until you act like Him.

I John 4:8 will explain this.

He that loveth not knoweth not God; for God is love.
— *I John 4:8*

"He that loveth not..." How do I love not? By not loving others like Jesus loved me on the cross. When you don't love like Jesus loved you on the cross, you don't know God. "He that loveth not knoweth not God." When you don't act like the cross, you don't know God. When you can't let go of how people have mistreated you, you don't know God. God gave the Jews prosperity and blessing. He delivered them, came through for them, and Jesus still said they did not know Him because they couldn't act like Him. Did you notice in Verse 8 that John never said, "He that loveth not is not born again"? So you can be born again and still not know God. He only said, "When you don't love, you don't *know* Him." He didn't say anything about being born again in that verse, but He did in Verse 7. You can have love down on the inside of you and not be walking in that love. You aren't living that love out.

Beloved, let us love one another: for love is of God; and every one that loveth is born of God, and knoweth God.
— *I John 4:7*

Look at I John 5:20.

And we know that the Son of God is come, and hath given us an understanding, that we may know him that is true, and we are in him that is true, even in his Son Jesus Christ. This is the true God, and eternal life.
— *I John 5:20*

"And we know that the Son of God is come..." Why? So He can die on the cross? No! So He can give us an understanding, that we may know Him that is true. When you are in Jesus, you are in the true God — and we are in Him that is true. You see, you have to know that when you are in Jesus, you are in the true God. "...and we are in him that is true, even in his Son Jesus Christ." Then it says, "This is the true God..." You don't have to look anywhere else. The understanding Jesus brought us is the true God and eternal life. I don't have to wonder if I know the true God. I don't have to be guessing what the true God knew, because I can look at Jesus and get an understanding of Him. Then I have an understanding of the true God. Not a God I don't know, but a God I do know in Christ Jesus. We are supposed to know that Jesus came to give us an understanding. We are to know this so we can know Him that is true. We are to know this so what we do will work, God's power will show up, and we will overcome every situation that gets in our way; because we know the true God. We aren't just trying to make this thing work. We have an understanding about love and how much God loved us in Jesus. He's always on our side. If God be for me then who can be against me? If love be for me — what He did for me on the cross — then who can be against me?

He that hath my commandments, and keepth them, he it is that loveth me: and he that loveth me shall be loved of my Father, and I will love him, and will manifest myself to him.
— John 14:21

A lot of people say that I focus too much on Jesus and that I take away from God; but, if you are honoring the Son, you are honoring God. I'm preaching God when I preach Jesus. You aren't supposed to preach God, you are supposed to preach Jesus, and that is preaching God. Does it say in this verse, "He that hath Moses' commandments and keepth them"? No! I'm not against Moses' commandments. I'm just saying that Jesus didn't teach that we are to have Moses' commandments. That's my point. I'm trying to point you to Christ. Every time I teach, I talk about Jesus. Then when I get through, I talk about Jesus again. Then when I get through there, I talk about Jesus again; and again and again and again.

Chapter 5

JESUS — THE PICTURE OF GOD

I want to help you see more clearly the revelation of why Jesus is right. You have to hear this word over and over so that the Spirit can bring to light that you can trust Jesus; the works He did were from God and every word He spoke out of His mouth was from God. Jesus said,

...the words that I speak unto you, they are spirit, and they are life.
— *John 6:63*

You can know that Jesus came from God, He was always with God, and He was the perfect image of God. He was the very likeness of God. Christ was everything God is, everything God says, and everything God does; exactly. There is no God outside of Jesus. Jesus is the only way we can know God and we know God the same way Jesus knew God, by His love. The only way you are going to know this love is by acting like it. You aren't going to know God from learning. You only know God by acting and obeying what Jesus taught you. When the opportunity arises, instead of getting mad, love like Jesus loved you; now you have grown Spiritually. You have matured. You've seen His power. Things will quit bothering you. I haven't been offended in over 19 years. Nobody! I'm not bragging on me, I'm just teaching you what this has done in my life. That doesn't mean I don't get angry. It doesn't mean I don't like the way someone does me and head the wrong direction every now and then, but I never go where my feelings lead me. When this Word is on your mind and in your heart, it catches you and constrains you. You won't go the way the flesh or the enemy wants to take you. You will become sensitive to God. I walk very tender before God. I can't hurt people. I can't be mean and ugly to people. I can't do it; no matter what they do to me. I've passed that test in my love walk. The more you walk in this, the more you become like God, the more you become like Jesus. Nothing bothered Him; nothing ever got Him out of Love.

All things are delivered to me of my Father: and no man knoweth who the Son is, but the Father; and who the Father is, but the Son, and he to whom the Son will reveal him.
— *Luke 10:22*

Who is "no man"? It's everyone that has ever been born on earth. He did not say that some of the kings and some of the prophets really knew God. He knocked everybody out. Man has tried to know God from his brain, or intellect, and that's wrong. He has no power to really love when he is mistreated. It's a struggle. But, it's the easiest thing in the world for me to forgive. I hear Christians say, "It's just hard to love some people." They get that from their intellect, from their senses, from their feelings. Jesus didn't teach that. When you get Jesus' Words in you, and let Him reveal the Father to you, *it's not hard.* Jesus never teaches anything that is hard. Everything He teaches is *easy.* You have to get that revelation in your thinking and down in your spirit. Jesus never gives you something hard. Peace comes with everything He tells you to do. Strength comes with everything He tells you to do. Grace and the ability to do it comes with everything Jesus tells you to do. Nothing God says is hard. You have to quit thinking and talking that it is hard so it will quit being hard. It's so easy just to forgive and forget because the more you renew your mind to this and obey; the easier it becomes. It gets so easy.

The Lord is taking His church to a place where we become so Jesus-minded — what Jesus taught, said, and did minded — that when somebody stands up and we don't hear the voice of the good Shepherd, we will say, "That's not my Master talking to me." That's not love when you tell me God is going to punish me and God is taking me through this to teach me something. Jesus didn't teach that, nor did He do that to His disciples.

In Luke 22:31 you will see what Jesus did when people were all twisted up.

And the Lord said, Simon, Simon, behold, Satan hath desired to have you, that he may sift you as wheat:
— *Luke 22:31*

Why did the devil want to sift Peter? The Amplified Bible says he wanted to sift all of the disciples — not just Simon, all of them.

Simon, Simon (Peter), listen! Satan has asked excessively that [all of] you be given up to him [out of the power and keeping of God], that he might sift [all of] you like grain, But I have prayed especially for you [Peter], that your [own] faith may not fail; and when you yourself have turned again, strengthen and establish your brethren.
— *Luke 22:31-32 (AMP)*

Always look in the Word for answers. Never think. Anytime you are using your brain it's not the Holy Spirit. The Holy Spirit can bring it up *to* your brain but you can't ever conjure it up *with* your brain. Some people need to re-discipline themselves to listen and start looking to the Holy Spirit to bring them answers instead of thinking up stuff that isn't right.

Look at why Satan desired to sift him in Luke 22:24.

And there was also a strife among them, which of them should be accounted the greatest.
— *Luke 22:24*

People in church today are fussing and arguing about doctrine and what they think the Bible means, instead of saying, "Jesus said, Jesus taught, Jesus did." There is no argument there. There is no debate when the Master says something. This is the only way we are going to get in unity. We aren't going to get in unity following Paul or anybody else in the Bible. We aren't ever going to agree on everything about the Bible. It's not going to happen. But, we can agree on what Jesus taught, what Jesus said, and what Jesus did. That's where the church has to come into unity. The Master said!

A new commandment I give unto you, That ye love one another; as I have loved you, that ye also love one another.
— ***John 13:34***

There is no debate here.

Jesus said,

...I am the way, the truth, and the life: no man cometh unto the Father, but by me.
— ***John 14:6***

There's no debate on that.

Jesus said,

All things are delivered to me of my Father: and no man knoweth who the Son is, but the Father; and who the Father is, but the Son, and he to whom the Son will reveal him.
— ***Luke 10:22***

There's no debate about that. Jesus said if He doesn't reveal the Father to you, you can't know Him. There's no debate on that because the Master said it.

Jesus said in John 15:7,

If ye abide in me, and my words abide in you, ye shall ask what ye will, and it shall be done unto you.
— ***John 15:7***

Jesus said, "My words." Not the Bible, but "My words." That doesn't mean that you throw away the Bible or the Old Testament. What Jesus taught was bringing truth and life from God that nobody else knew about. You have to get His Words in you so that this can work in your life. You are never to let the apostles or anybody else take you away from the foundation of the Words of Jesus Christ — the nature, character, and authority that was in Him. Nobody, in any book, or in any teaching, is to ever take you away from Him. Nobody! I don't care what kind of ministry they have. I don't care how "big" they are. They should never be able to take you away from Jesus. Brother Hagin taught me that if he doesn't prove something by the Word, don't accept it. I teach the same thing everywhere I go. I am a Word man. I have heard ministers teach that the Gospels are not for us, that we need to focus on the Pauline letters. Now, there is a measure of truth in this, but it isn't *the* truth because Jesus didn't say that. There is some truths that we need to get from the Pauline letters but that's not *the* truth because the Master didn't say that. He said, "My words." There is something in Jesus' words that we have to have. It's not everything; but it is the foundation for everything. Everything else must be build upon His Words. Nothing should ever takes us away from what Jesus taught, what Jesus said, what Jesus did; how He loved us on the cross; His commandments and His teachings. All our doctrine should be built on Jesus' teachings. If you are not content with what Jesus taught, then you aren't in fellowship with God. Jesus is the only way to God and He's the only way you are going to walk with God. He's the only way you are going to get God revealed to you. You can't have fellowship with God outside of Jesus and obeying His teachings.

Can you see why the devil wanted to sift them as wheat? Let's see what Love did. Did He say, "Why, you big old dummies, you didn't have any business getting in strife. I hope the devil knocks all of your heads off and teaches you a good lesson." No! Love is in Verse 32.

But I have prayed for thee, that thy faith fail not: and when thou art converted, strengthen thy brethren.
— Luke 22:32

Jesus said, "I have prayed." He wants to help us when we get in trouble. Even when we have sinned He wants to love us, help us, and bring us out. He doesn't want the devil doing anything to us. If He wanted the devil to teach us something, He would not have prayed. "But I have prayed for thee, that thy faith fail not." Jesus doesn't ever want your faith to fail. What was their faith in? They believed that God sent Jesus. Your faith must be in the same thing and let that faith grow. God sent Christ to reveal who God is. You can find this all through the Scriptures. It's amazing! As you go back and read and study now, this will open up to you. Five years from now it will still be opening up even more to you. Anything that is eternal life never stops. Revelations that stop, are cut off and don't go any further should be questioned whether they are true. Truth just keeps going and going and going.

Who is the image of the invisible God, the firstborn of every creature:
— *Colossians 1:15*

Who was the firstborn of every creature? Jesus. Who is the visible image of the invisible God? Jesus. God has always been invisible to man so He stepped out of the invisible, stepped into Jesus, and became visible. The New Living Translation says,

Christ is the visible image of the invisible God...
— *Colossians 1:15 (NLT)*

Jesus is your picture of God. He is the best picture of God we will ever get. He's not going to be wrong about God in anything because He acted just like God. Job said in Job 1:21, "...the Lord gave, and the Lord hath taken away; blessed be the name of the Lord." Well, "Blessed be the name of the Lord" is good. And, "The Lord gave" is good. But Jesus didn't teach, "The Lord hath taken away." Christians have believed that God is everything ever said about Him; that He will get you, take from you, and take you through hell. It's the devil that takes you through hell — God doesn't need to help him! When you get depressed, God doesn't need to add to your depression. He delivers you from it. God is love. He isn't anything else. If you were to squeeze an orange, you wouldn't get any apple juice out of it. I don't care how hard you squeeze that orange, all that is going to come out is orange juice. Every time you squeeze God — you can squeeze Him at the top and squeeze Him at the bottom and squeeze Him in the middle — all that is going to ooze out of Him is Love. All that is going to come out of Him is Jesus. All that is going to come out of Him is forgiving you and setting you free. You can't squeeze anything else out of God because God squeezed Jesus out of Him;

that's the only thing that comes out of God — Jesus and His love on the cross. So, every time you go through some kind of trouble, go squeeze God and you will squeeze out Jesus. When people mistreat you, all that God wants to do for them is love them and help them come out of how they did you. He doesn't have anything else to squeeze out to them but Jesus. Now they could get some death but it's not God's will. His will is that we don't get death. He can't change what He did in Jesus. He can't reverse how He loved us in Christ. I don't care what anybody has done to you; God can't get them because He didn't get you.

Colossians 1:15 says in The New Living Translation, "Christ is the visible image of the invisible God." Aren't you glad we can know the truth? Aren't you glad we don't have to wonder whether God did those things that the Old Testament said He did — burning everybody up and having a barbecue? You need to take hold of Who Jesus is so you can discern what is of God and what isn't. Some people think I don't love the Old Testament but I really do. I love all of God's Word. I'm just not *following* the Old Testament. It's exciting to see what God did in Old Testament, but I discern what God did and didn't do back then through Jesus. I know God permitted those awful things to happen; He did not commit them.

At one time we lived in a one-bedroom apartment and we had cold air coming in on my wife's side of the bed. She told me she wasn't going to sleep there anymore because it was cold. I said, "Well, I don't want to be over there either." Guess who started sleeping over there? Me! And it was cold. The covers didn't stay on very well at night and I would shiver from the cold; we ended up getting a little heater. I set it on the floor near my side of the bed so that the heat would stop the cold air from getting on me. Our son was two years old at that time and I didn't want him to touch the heater and get burned. I sat down with him in front of the heater and touched it saying, "Hot, hot!" Then I put his finger up close to it where he could feel the heat and I said, "Hot, burn!" At that moment I remembered I was boiling him a bottle and I heard the water boiling over on the stove. I jumped up and ran in the kitchen to take it off the stove. While I was taking it off the burner, I heard a scream. Guess what my son did. He touched the heater. I ran in the bedroom and kissed his finger, I bound the devil, I rebuked the pain — I did everything I could think of; it hurt me to see him hurting like that. It was blistering. I put butter on it. I put ice on it. I kissed it. I prayed over it. I bound the devil again. I was just a young Christian man, and I did everything I knew to do. But here is my question to you: Did I want my son to learn that the heater was hot from my words or from the pain? From my words, of course. Did I permit my son to get burned? Yes. Why? Because, he had a choice. I gave him my word and he had a choice as to which one he was going to do. The pain didn't come from me, it came from his choice. The same goes for God; people blame Him for the pain in their lives when it's coming from their choices. God loves you. Where was the love in my son's situation? Showing my son the right way. Sometimes that's all God can do for you — tell you the right way.

Then spake Jesus again unto them, saying, I am the light of the world: he that followeth me shall not walk in darkness, but shall have the light of life.
— John 8:12

You might do something; not following Jesus, and get in a mess. Then the devil comes along and writes you a note; puts it on your situation saying, "God did this to you. He's punishing you because you've been bad." Listen, you were punished by your own actions. God doesn't need to punish you any more. You need some love. People think God wanted all those bad things to come upon Job.

And his sons went and feasted in their houses, every one his day; and sent and called for their three sisters to eat and to drink with them. And it was so, when the days of their feasting were gone about, that Job sent and sanctified them, and rose up early in the morning, and offered burnt offerings according to the number of them all: for Job said, It may be that my sons have sinned, and cursed God in their hearts. Thus did Job continually.
— Job 1:4-5

God did not ask the devil to get Job. Job's fear opened the door to the devil. He was afraid that his sons had sinned and cursed God in their hearts so he was offering God burnt offerings for them continually. God didn't have anything to do with it. God has nothing to do with fear. God only gets involved with faith in Jesus. When you are in fear, the devil has a right to come. When you are in faith, God has a right to come. God only permitted what Job chose; he was in fear about his children.

The devil didn't even know the hedge was down around Job; because he can't be everywhere at once. Notice what the devil said to God,

Hast not thou made an hedge about him, and about his house, and about all that he hath on every side? thou hast blessed the work of his hands, and his substance is increased in the land.
— Job 1:10

While Job was in faith, the devil couldn't get to him. Why did God tell the devil he couldn't kill Job? Because, Job had not sown a sin that was worthy of death. The devil could only make him reap what he had sown. God permitted what Job chose; that's what he is going to do in your life because He's the same in Jesus. Galatians 6:7-8 says,

Be not deceived; God is not mocked: for whatsoever a man soweth, that shall he also reap. For he that soweth to his flesh shall of the flesh reap corruption;..."
— Galatians 6:7-8

If you sow in the flesh, you will reap in the flesh. If you are mean to people, all that will come back to you. Sometimes it's not always what you have sown. Sometimes the devil just comes to harass you. There are times demons are assigned to come for a season just to harass and bug you. You've got to learn to resist that. What do you do when you get harassed? Look at James 4:7.

Submit yourselves therefore to God. Resist the devil, and he will flee from you.
— James 4:7

The only God you know is Jesus, so who are you submitting to? Jesus. Submit yourselves therefore to the God that was in Jesus and resist the devil, because Jesus told you He gave you authority over him. You need Jesus' teachings to know what James is talking about. You are to resist the devil and put him on the run. Make him run with terror. When you know what Jesus taught, your response to him is, "No, no, no, you can't do me like this. I am not in your family anymore. God loves me and there is nothing you can do about it. If I mess up He will still love me." You see, we haven't stood up to the devil and laughed at him. Jesus has whipped him. Quit talking about what the devil is doing and start talking about what God is doing; what love is doing. Every time the Bible says God, think about the love that God is in Jesus on the cross. Put that right there. You will get more revelation. Look at Matthew 13:34.

All these things spake Jesus unto the multitude in parables; and without a parable spake he not unto them:
— Matthew 13:34

Why was Jesus always talking in parables? He talked in parables so that those who didn't have an ear to hear couldn't understand. He's still speaking in parables today. That's why people don't understand Him; they don't want to. This teaching will stick to the people that really want God like glue. But, you have got to be saying, "I want this," or it will be just another teaching. If you are saying, "I want this, I'm going for this, I'm getting a hold of this, I want to love like Jesus more, I want to be like Jesus more," that stir you up and give you insight; taking you further in the Scriptures. It should redirect your thinking. It will help you, strengthen you, and encourage you; leading you right to Jesus.

Jesus said in many places, "If any man have ears to hear, let him hear." The word "hear" in the Greek means "to hear effectively so as to perform or grant what is spoken." Jesus isn't asking people to listen and then see if they want to do it. He is saying, "Hear what I say to you and do it. Whatever I say, grant and perform it." If you tell me it's hard to love some people, you aren't going to do it. You aren't going to walk in this. When Jesus tells you to do something, don't challenge Him and tell Him you lack the ability. Do it. Perform it. Grant it. He will never tell you to do something or command you to do something you can't do. He's not unjust. He's just and righteous in everything. If He says it, you can do it.

That it might be fulfilled which was spoken by the prophet, saying, I will open my mouth in parables; I will utter things which have been kept secret from the foundation of the world.
— *Matthew 13:35*

Jesus knew what had been kept secret since the foundation of the world about God. That's why no man knew this; that's why if you don't start taking Jesus at His Word, you will never walk in this. Never. Why? He says you won't. If you keep living in your thinking and how you feel, He is never going to show this to you. He doesn't have feelings. Now, God does have compassion and affection for us; to be there for us in Jesus. Jesus is the affection of God. It's not a feeling.

Let's go back and see what a prophet of old said and get some insight.

Give ear, O my people, to my law: incline your ears to the words of my mouth.
— *Psalm 78:1*

Now, I don't need the Old Testament prophets to tell me that Jesus is real; but who else could David be talking about here? I already know Jesus is real with out David. Paul needed the Old Testament to help the Jews know that Jesus was the Messiah, but the Gentiles didn't need that. God will show you His love. He will manifest Himself to you and show you how real He is. Jesus will touch you in a way that you will know He is real when you call on Him out of a sincere heart. He will be there for you and will help you. You don't need any more proof that the Lord is real after you have been born of God. It's time for you to walk with Him and obey what Jesus said.

I used to read this Psalm before I received this revelation and I believed this was God speaking. But look at it very carefully. "Give ear, O my people, to my law: incline your ears to the words of my mouth." Who can see God's mouth? No one. Who then was talking here? It was His Word, before it became flesh, telling us, "Get ready to listen to me, the words that come out of my mouth." This is prophetic for us today. Can you see that this is Jesus? If this is not enough for you then look at Verse 2.

I will open my mouth in a parable: I will utter dark sayings of old.
— Psalm 78:2

That settles it right there. That's Jesus. Now what is "dark sayings of old"? I looked that up in the Hebrew and it means "a puzzle or riddle or parable." The Hebrew gave an example of Samson. The riddle that came by Samson was so complicated that no one could decipher it without inside information. Samson gave the kings a riddle, a parable, a puzzle and they couldn't figure it out until they went to Samson's wife and threatened to kill her and her family if she didn't give them the inside information so they could answer to the riddle. Jesus is the inside information of God, and without getting close to Jesus you can't find out how to get this thing unraveled in your life. You have to get close to Jesus so He can reveal the puzzle to you, open it up and give you inside information about how much God loves you and what God did for you in Jesus on the cross. I can show you over and over again in the Old Testament where Jesus spoke and said get ready, incline your ears to the words of my mouth. It's all through Proverbs. When you read, "Incline your ears to the words of my mouth," that's Jesus saying get ready to listen to what is going to come out of His mouth. He says it over and over.

It's got to line up with the Master — the character and authority of God. I'm not talking about what's going to happen in Revelation. You say, "Isn't God going to come down here and destroy?" God is going to come down here and kick the devil! Love always renders darkness powerless. He's going to come and whip darkness. He's light. You get the picture of that on the cross. Jesus disarmed the principalities and powers that were raised against us.

And having spoiled principalities and powers, he made a shew of them openly, triumphing over them in it.
— Colossians 2:15

You are to do the same thing. You are to disarm the devil the same way Jesus did — by your love walk and your faith. You can't just say, "Jesus did it." No, you have to learn to act just like Him so what He did can operate in you. It doesn't work because He did it. It works when you do it just like He did. If it just worked because Jesus went to the cross and died for everybody, how come all Christians aren't loving and kind? Because, they aren't acting like it. You don't get healed because He healed you on the cross. Either the gifts have to work or you have to be in faith.

Look at John 2:1-5.

And the third day there was a marriage in Cana of Galilee; and the mother of Jesus was there: And both Jesus was called, and his disciples, to the marriage. And when they wanted wine, the mother of Jesus saith unto him, They have no wine. Jesus saith unto her, Woman, what have I to do with thee? Mine hour is not yet come. His mother saith unto the servants, Whatsoever he saith unto you, do it.

— John 2:1-5

You need to get the same revelation Mary had: "...Whatsoever he saith unto you, do it." Don't be asking Him why we have to fill these pots up with water. Don't be asking Him why we have to love our enemies. Don't be asking Jesus why. Just do it. When He tells you to forgive when you stand praying, don't ask Him why. "Well, I don't want to forgive what they did to me." You aren't reverencing the true living God in Jesus when you question Him in any way. That's what's wrong with people's brains. They want to figure out why. You can't walk with Jesus and use your brain. You can't know the love of Christ unless you pass your knowledge; it's not going to make sense — all of us were guilty and He died in our place; having done nothing wrong. That is never going to make sense. It's never going to make sense that He died for ungodly people. Your brain is never going to be able to figure that out. It's got to pass your brain. When you see His love in your heart, you will be filled with all the fullness of God. If you want to know the love of Christ, you have to pass your knowledge.

Jesus' mother had a revelation: whatever He says to you; do it. Guess what kind of revelation she had. This is it: everything Jesus says always happens. Most Christians don't believe that. Jesus talks to me when His anointing is on me, and people question it. They say, "You mean if I jump I will be healed?" Jesus tells me to tell some people that. They question Jesus because they aren't used to obeying. They are used to doing whatever they want in life. Then they just sort of bring Jesus in; receiving eternal life to make sure they are going to heaven, but they haven't ever followed Him. Ever! They never read the red words and say, "I'm going to live them." My guess would be that 95% of Christians are in that boat, in every church. They are good people. God has blessed them and done a lot of good things for them because He will show you His love even if you don't love like Him. He's still going to be God. God doesn't wait until you get all of your ducks in a row before He blesses you. If He did, He wouldn't bless any of us. He's love. In every crack you give God, He shoots up His love. Where He can't come up, He can't come up; He wants to because He can't be anything but love. Every time you give God some room, He's going to love. Where you don't give Him room, you have stopped Him, but He still wants to be love.

Look at Romans 8:35.

Who shall separate us from the love of Christ? Shall tribulation, or distress, or persecution, or famine, or nakedness, or peril, or sword?
— Romans 8:35

Who is going to separate you from the love of Christ? Nothing can separate you from the love of Christ except your disobedience. You can never stop Him from the way He loved you on the cross. The cross and what He did for us stays there and waits until faith comes and accesses it. It can never change. It can never be altered. If you call on Him in faith, He's got to deliver you. He's got to heal you. He's got to prosper you. He's got to set you free because He's already done it. He's already loved you. He can't change how He loved you on the cross. However, you do have something to do with it. If you didn't, then the cross should have made everyone get saved and live right. It can't do that. You have to cooperate with God. Let's keep reading in Romans 8.

As it is written, For thy sake we are killed all the day long; we are accounted as sheep for the slaughter.
— Romans 8:36

David said that. Any time you see "it is written," they are quoting the Old Testament. This isn't Jesus talking. This is His apostle by the Holy Spirit talking. You need to look for Jesus; Him crucified and resurrected in these verses. Always look for Jesus. Don't look for Paul. Look for the revelation of Jesus from Paul.

Nay, in all these things we are more than conquerors through him that loved us.
— Romans 8:37

No! You are more than a conqueror. Where did Paul get that revelation that we are more than conquerors? Paul got that through the revelation he had from Jesus on the cross. He got it from Jesus and how we got loved, and he brought us the revelation that we are more than conquerors through Him that loved us on the cross. The more you see that love, the more revelation you will get. It works because it is in line with Jesus and the cross. He knew that we were more than conquerors through Him that loved us.

Look at this verse in the New Living Translation.

No, despite all these things, overwhelming victory is ours through Christ, who loved us.
— Romans 8:37 (NLT)

Overwhelming victory! Not just a little victory. Overwhelming victory is ours through Christ, who loved us. This is our victory. This is our life. This is where we conquer and win in Christ. Let's read on.

For I am persuaded, that neither death, nor life, nor angels, nor principalities, nor powers, nor things present, nor things to come

Nor height, nor depth, nor any other creature, shall be able to separate us from the love of God, which is in Christ Jesus our Lord.
— Romans 8:38-39

Notice that Paul didn't say *you* were persuaded. He said *he* was persuaded. What was he persuaded about? That neither death, nor life, nor angels, nor principalities, nor powers, nor things present, nor things to come, nor height, nor depth, nor any other creature shall be able to separate us from the love of God which is in Christ Jesus. That love isn't anywhere else. There's no picture of that love anywhere else. Nothing we do can ever stop that love, how Jesus loved us on the cross. Now, we can stop His love from manifesting through our rebellion towards obeying Him. God can't love you when you are being mean. He can only love you to bring you out of being like that. He can't love you so you can keep acting ugly. One time I was witnessing to a homosexual and I told him God loved him. He replied, "I know God loves me. It doesn't matter what I do or how I am. I know God still loves me." I said to him, "No, He doesn't." He doesn't love when He can't change you. His love never loves wrong. His love wants to love that homosexual out of being like that anymore. His love did something about him being in that state. His love makes you free; His love makes you act like Jesus. That's God's love. It's not so you can keep doing what you are doing. That's not His love. It's not His love for you to stay like you are. His love is for you to come progressively to the light; obeying Jesus in a greater level every day.

Look at Romans 8:38-39 in the New Living Translation.

And I am convinced that nothing can ever separate us from his love. Death can't, and life can't. The angels can't, and the demons can't. Our fears for today, our worries about tomorrow, and even the powers of hell can't keep God's love away. Whether we are high above the sky or in the deepest ocean, nothing in all creation will ever be able to separate us from the love of God that is revealed in Christ Jesus our Lord.
— Romans 8:38-39 (NLT)

This wasn't Jesus speaking. This was Paul's faith by the Holy Spirit in Jesus. *You* must also become convinced. Paul was already convinced. *You* have to get your faith in Jesus' teachings so that *you* can know this. The red words will cause you to talk like this. Even when you are going through the worst time in your life, it can't keep God's love away. God's love will find a way to get down in the cracks of the hell you are going through and pull you up out of there. God will come down to hell with you and get you out of it. Love doesn't say, "Get yourself together now." No, love already came down and made a way for you to get yourself together.

Let's sum it up. No matter what you go through, love can come and rescue you. God can never quit loving you in Jesus no matter what you go through and no matter how many times you mess up. His love still loves you the same way it did before you messed up. It's there waiting to do what love does; bring you out, heal you, and set you free. It just stands there and waits until you activate it.

Look at John 14:21 for the picture of what I have just said from Jesus so you will see that it is lining up with the Word. I don't teach anything that I can't show you Jesus taught, said, and did. Almost everything the New Testament writers taught was what Jesus taught, said, and did. They didn't teach anything else.

He that hath my commandments, and keepth them, he it is that loveth me: and he that loveth me shall be loved of my Father, and I will love him, and will manifest myself to him.
—John 14:21

Everybody doesn't love Jesus. They are lying if they say they do. They are putting on a façade because they are afraid somebody will find out that they don't. Guess what, those that really walk with God already know. The more light you walk in, the more you can see through the façade people have up. You don't see it in order to condemn them, but you do see it. The Holy Spirit will show you these people, not to condemn them, but so that you can pray for them, help them, love them, and bring them out of it.

Jesus said; the person that has His commandments and keeps them; he is the one who loves Him. The feelings you have for God because He has been good to you are just feelings. Feelings are not love. Real Love for Jesus is when you hear what He says and do it. No matter how you feel; that's how you love Him. You don't love Him any other way, because He didn't teach you to love Him any other way.

Jesus said, "...and I will love him." Who is "him"? Now, don't think. Go back to the beginning of the verse. There are two things here — first, the person that has His commandments, and second, the person that keeps them. That is the person Jesus is going to love. No one else. When Jesus loves you, He empowers you to conquer what's in your way. He doesn't love everybody to empower them to conquer. He can't go against His Word. He might send us to go help those who cannot conquer, but He isn't going to. He's only going to love those people who take His words, His commandments and teachings, and do them.

Look what else He said He was going to do: "...I will love him, and will manifest Myself to him." When you give your heart to Jesus, He manifests Himself to you. When you made a decision to start reading your Bible, praying, and doing what He said, He touched you. If you quit doing what He says, He will stop. Even that which you seem to have will be taken away from you. You can't play with this.

Jesus said, "...I will manifest Myself to him." Who is "him"? The one that has His commandments and keeps them. These are the only people Jesus is going to manifest Himself to; no one else on earth. Who are the only people that Jesus is going to love? Now, you must remember, Jesus loves everybody in what He did on the cross, but He does not love and manifest Himself to everybody. He only loves everybody on the cross in what He did for them, but unless they obey Him He doesn't get to show them His love. He doesn't need to show you how to win when you don't want to win. He isn't going to anoint you so you can go watch TV all the time. Why? It's junk. It's garbage. Most programs are full of people that are lusting, sinning, and hurting people's lives. If you think that's funny; you aren't walking with Jesus. When you start obeying Jesus you will hate that stuff.

The Lord isn't telling you to quit everything you are doing. Jesus is simply saying, "Lay your life down and follow Me." When you do this; the desire to do the things that displease Him will stop. There might even be areas in your life that you don't know aren't right. When you walk with Him, you will lose the taste for the world and darkness. The light of His Holiness will get brighter in you; creating a desire in you to want to please Him and not the devil and this world. You have to want this. Many times I have seen a wife wanting this and a husband that doesn't, or vice versa. It sure is good when they both want this and pray and read the Word together, but you don't find that very often. In most situations - one will want to jump, one won't. One will want to shout, and the other won't. Why don't both of you shout? How come both of you can't be crazy about Jesus? How come both of you can't get up and dance?

Look at Verse 21 in the Amplified Bible.

The person who has My commands and keeps them is the one who [really] loves Me; and whoever [really] loves Me will be loved by My Father, and I [too] will love him and will show (reveal, manifest) Myself to him. [I will let Myself be clearly seen by him and make Myself real to him.]
— John 14:21 (AMP)

He is going to get to show Himself strong in those people that have His commandments and keep them because they are obeying Jesus. Jesus goes on to say, "I will let Myself be clearly seen by him and make Myself real to him." Do you know what is going to be made real to you? How He loved you will be made real to you, because you are obeying His commandment of loving one another the way He loved you. You will clearly see what He did on the cross; causing it to work in your life the same way. Jesus whipped the devil on the cross; the reality of that in your life whips the devil too. Let's go back to John 14.

Judas saith unto him, not Iscariot, Lord, how is it that thou wilt manifest thyself unto us, and not unto the world? Jesus answered and said unto him, If a man love me, he will keep my words: and my

Father will love him, and we will come unto him, and make our abode with him.
— *John 14:22-23*

Do you know what the word "commandments" means? "Words". The words "commandments" and "words" mean the same thing. Do you know what the word "sayings" means? "Words" and "commandments". Do you know what the word "teachings" means? "Commandments", "words" and "sayings".

Look at I John 1:3-4.

And hereby we do know that we know him, if we keep his commandments. He that saith, I know him, and keepeth not his commandments, is a liar, and the truth is not in him. But whoso keepeth his word, in him verily is the love of God perfected: hereby know we that we are in him.
— *I John 2:3-5*

When you obey loving like Jesus, love is matured in you. Where did John get that? From Jesus. This is what Jesus was teaching in John 21. John was listening to what Jesus said. He goes on to say,

He that saith he abideth in him ought himself also so to walk, even as he walked.
— *I John 2:6*

John had the revelation that we can be just like Jesus. Most Christians don't believe this. Why would Jesus tell us to love the same way He loved if we couldn't do it? We can. That's why Paul said,

I can do all things through Christ which strengtheneth me.
— *Philippians 4:13*

He knew he could do all things through what Jesus taught, said, and did, because Jesus was going to give him the strength to do it. You might quote that from your head, but Paul had the revelation that he had heard from Jesus. He knew he could do it. It doesn't say *you* can.

That isn't Jesus talking. It doesn't say *you* can do all things through Christ. Paul said, "I can." You also must get the revelation of faith in Jesus for yourself so that you can, too.

Go back to John 14:23.

Jesus answered and said unto him, If a man love me, he will keep my words...
— John 14:23

When you don't love Jesus, you stay mad at people. You talk about people you don't even know. You will take what your best friend told you, tell it to your spouse, and spread a rumor. If you were loving like Jesus you couldn't do that. Your excuse is, "Well, that's my best friend." Well, RAH, RAH, RAH!

...If a man love me, he will keep my words: and my Father will love him, and we will come unto him, and make our abode with him.
— John 14:23

Who is the Father going to love? Those who keeps Jesus' words. You might ask, "What do you mean? Doesn't God love everybody?" Yes, He does on the cross — but He isn't going to get to show everybody. Some people aren't going to have any joy or peace because Jesus isn't getting to give it to them. He could if they simply obeyed Him; forgiving themselves and those who did them wrong.

Jesus said, "...and my Father will love him, and *we* will come unto him, and make our abode with him." Jesus said, "and we...." Who is we? Jesus said, "...If a man love me, he will keep my words: and my Father will love him, and *we* will come..." Let's see; Jesus whipped the devil all by Himself. What is the devil going to do with the Father *and* the Son? He couldn't handle Jesus. What is he going to do with God and Jesus coming down and making their abode with *us*? How are we going to lose with the Father and the Son on our behalf, on our side, with us?

We! We! We will come and make our home, make our residence, make our permanent stay with those who love Jesus. He isn't talking about being born again. He's talking about the Presence of Love and Authority working in *your* life. It's going to reside in you. If you get mad at somebody and refuse to forgive, it isn't resident in you anymore. You are still saved, but the Father and the Son aren't making Their home in you, when you aren't obeying Jesus. When you really get this revelation, you will never stay mad at anybody because you will be afraid the Father and the Son aren't going to be there. That scares me; I want Them there. Some people sit in church and cry, "Why isn't God blessing me?" You aren't obeying Jesus, that's why! "Why don't I have any joy?" You aren't walking in love, that's why! God has made Himself to live in us. We aren't supposed to lose in *anything*. We have the Father and the Son. The devil hates this, but there is nothing he can do about it. That's why I can laugh, because I have the Father and the Son. What in the world is hell going to do about that? They couldn't handle Jesus. They couldn't keep Jesus in hell. What in the world are they going to do with God Almighty? What are you facing today that looks so big? What are you looking at that looks so hard? This will put a smile on your face! He wants to help you and love you. He wants to show you this love. He is tired of you suffering, tired of all that junk being in you, waking up every morning unhappy and oppressed by the devil. He is tired because He has made a way for you to be full of His joy and strength.

Remember that Jesus is **The Truth** and what Jesus said is **The Truth**. He loves you no matter what on the cross which is available for you to come out of everything that is wrong, but He isn't going to love you like you are so you can stay like that. That isn't His love. His love is POWER — it has to *do* something. It doesn't just love and do nothing. That's not God's love. That's not Jesus on the cross. Jesus on the cross does something for you.

PRAYER

Many people who call themselves Christians have only had a belief in Christ. When they were young they prayed a prayer, or someone told them to just believe and they would be saved. This has been such an error in the "Christian World." The Word of God does say that anyone who calls on the name of the Lord shall be saved, but there needs to be a change. Calling is laying your life down – totally surrendering.

I believe that as you have read this book you may have seen that you have not given your WHOLE LIFE to Jesus. You have believed on Him, but you have struggles that you just can't overcome. It is because you have not given your whole life to Jesus Christ. You have not made Jesus right and everyone else – including yourself – wrong. I want to give you an opportunity to surrender your whole life to Jesus Christ as Lord of your life, where you no longer have a voice when it comes to the teachings of Jesus. Pray this prayer out loud if you want to give up your life and really live for Him.

Dear Heavenly Father, I come to you in the name of Your Son Jesus Christ. I repent for the sin of unbelief. I have already believed on You, but never trusted You with my whole life – my whole heart. I lay down my life to serve You and follow You to do God's will. From this day forward whatever You tell me to do, Lord Jesus, I will do it. Satan, I take authority over you in the name of Jesus! You cannot have me, my mind, my body or my soul anymore! Loose me and let me go! I am going all the way with Jesus! No turning back – I am God's child and what rules my life from now on is what Jesus taught, said, and did on the cross. Thank you Lord Jesus! I'm going all the way with You! In Jesus name – AMEN! 5·6·22 3:50

Remember the day and time that you prayed this prayer and keep it in your heart – I guarantee you will see a change after today, if you meant what you prayed.

Jesus loves you and I love you – keep yourselves in the Love of God! Remember that every step outside of love is sin.